# the
# *Conscious*
# Leader

The ultimate guide to
leading a life worth living
through crises and beyond

Award-winning author of *The Million Dollar Handshake*

# the *Conscious* Leader

The ultimate guide to leading a life worth living through crises and beyond

CATHERINE MOLLOY

First published in 2021 by Dean Publishing
PO Box 119
Mt. Macedon, Victoria, 3441
Australia
deanpublishing.com

Copyright © Catherine Molloy

All rights reserved. No part of this publication may be reproduced, stored in a retrieval system or transmitted in any way or by any means, electronic, mechanical, photocopying, recording or otherwise, without the prior written permission of the publisher.

Cataloguing-in-Publication Data
National Library of Australia
Title: The Conscious Leader—The ultimate guide to leading a life worth living through crises and beyond
Edition: 1st edn
ISBN: 978-1-925452-33-4
Category: BUSINESS/Entrepreneurship/Leadership

The views and opinions expressed in this book are those of the author and do not necessarily reflect the official policy or position of any other agency, publisher, organization, employer or company. Assumptions made in the analysis are not reflective of the position of any entity other than the author(s)—and, these views are always subject to change, revision, and rethinking at any time.

The author, publisher or organizations are not to be held responsible for misuse, reuse, recycled and cited and/or uncited copies of content within this book by others.

*This book is dedicated to all the
aspiring leaders of the world.*

*The changemakers that want to
step into conscious leadership and
make a difference for themselves,
and for their friends, families, teams,
businesses, communities, and the planet.*

# CONTENTS

Introduction ................................................................. ix

Chapter 1: Leading Yourself ........................................... 1

Chapter 2: Being Conscious Of Emotional Intelligence ............. 53

Chapter 3: Lead With Purpose ................................... 105

Chapter 4: Language For Leadership ..........................141

Chapter 5: Leading Others .........................................179

Chapter 6: The Conscious Currency ..........................219

Acknowledgments ................................................... 241

About The Author .................................................... 243

Endnotes ................................................................. 245

Catherine is sharing more in her INTERACTIVE book.

See exclusive downloads, videos, audios and photos.

DOWNLOAD it now at
deanpublishing.com/consciousleader

# INTRODUCTION

## CONSCIOUSLY WALKING ONTO THE STAGE OF LIFE

I stepped onto the main stage as thousands of new faces stared at me. I smiled and waved to them like an old friend. My high heels tapped a confident rhythm as I walked towards the center of the stage. The anticipation I had before starting my talk was palpable; I love the intimacy of a face-to-face audience. There is something special in the way thousands of strangers can connect so personally in one room, it sends chills down my spine.

In 2017 I was hired to give a presentation at a large workplace conference in India. The subject was one of my favorites, "First Impressions," and it was time to make mine as the keynote speaker. Of course, the crowd expected me to nail a good first impression given the keynote topic and I wouldn't let them down. I smiled at the audience with warmth and poise.

They had paid thousands of dollars to hear me speak and I wanted it to be worth every cent—and more. I gave it my all, sharing the wealth of knowledge I had accumulated from decades of experience in business. I wanted them to walk away with not only great information, but also inspiration and practical strategies to make a difference in the world. I left it all on the stage as they say.

You see, I am driven with a crazy passion to create, support and encourage conscious leaders in this world. It's my calling in life and what I am here to do. Conscious leadership isn't something that I talk *about*, it's something I *live*. And I have discovered that *living it* is the essential ingredient to success. In fact, it's what makes life juicy and meaningful.

Now, back to the stage with thousands of people, the truth is—I didn't technically leave it all out on stage that day. I certainly gave it my all but I kept something back. Not because I was hiding something, but because I had a strict time limit and didn't want to spend too much time talking about "me" because this was about them, not me. I didn't want to be self-indulgent one iota. My goal was to give the audience workable tools and strategies that they could walk away with and apply immediately.

What I didn't share was my personal journey, my deepest and most private story. It was a conscious decision not to share it back then but today I make a different choice: this time I want to share my story, the truth and the battle behind my smile and successful image.

It was only recently that I realized many people on the speaking circuit and in the audience only saw me as successful. They knew my book *The Million Dollar Handshake* or saw me on stage and assumed that it was just one success after another and I had some sort of golden secret.

The truth is, it wasn't one success after another. It was hard work, steep learning curves and hustle. But yes, there is a golden secret—and that's what I would like to share in this book: the true secrets that created *all* of my success. Are you ready?

## THE CRISIS, THE COLLAPSE AND THE CONQUERING

In 2008 the Global Financial Crisis hit. Those three innocuous letters, "GFC" upended my life, pouring the contents of my beautiful existence onto the ground in ruins. It ran with the swift current of a wildfire burning our investments with reckless abandon and leaving us with charred remains.

## INTRODUCTION

After it roared through my life, my husband John and I were swamped in debt. One million dollars of our hard-earned money literally disappeared in a blink. With it, went life as I knew it.

Before the GFC, I was swimming in the life I had created. You could say, it was the life of my dreams: a beautiful husband, three incredible kids and a successful career. Now, don't get me wrong, there were struggles and challenges, I am human after all, but I was living my ideal existence and didn't intend on stopping anytime soon.

We had worked so hard to build our dream life, that when the GFC came and swept it away, I felt more than ripped off. It had been such an enduring climb to reach the pinnacle of our life that I was blindsided when it looked like we had to start over again.

Sure, there were many other devastated people like us, but with three kids in private schools and my back against the wall, I was only thinking of how to survive. It was time to hustle and hustle hard.

Hustling wasn't entirely new to me. I had started my working career in service for the corporate banking sector and became deeply involved in learning about body language and its influence on people. The more I learned about people, the more interested I became. Sales skills and body language became my secret obsession. It wasn't the actual sale I was chasing, it was the avid interest in what made people tick, what made people feel comfortable, what made people conscious, and how I could best serve them. Applying this, *"how may I serve you?"* philosophy wasn't just a sales technique either, it was a true, caring intention that I held for every customer I worked with.

Before too long, I was topping sales in the industry and exceeding any KPIs set. The company took notice and gave me further training and education so that I could train staff and boost the bank's customer service teams. I loved my job and soon accepted a transfer working at the bank's commercial center for their multi-million-dollar clients, and undertaking some legal work for them.

Luckily for me, it wasn't all work and no play. Through work I met John, the love of my life and we quickly realized we were meant to be. Both young, blonde and in love, we were nicknamed "Ken and Barbie" by our work colleagues.

As our relationship grew serious, I broached the subject of kids. I had decided not to have children and told John my plans. He simply answered; "It's okay, I can't have children either," and we settled that elephant-in-the-room on the spot. "Well, that was easy," I thought to myself. Children weren't on my radar but traveling the world and enjoying life with John certainly was.

Then—I fell pregnant (surprise!) and all my preconceived notions about having children melted away. I understood what Woody Allen meant when he said, "If you want *to* make God laugh, tell him *about* your plans."

When I asked John why he had thought that he couldn't have children he said, "Well, I hadn't had any!" His strange reply made me delve deeper into behaviors and personalities, always learning more.

Thankfully, I've always been able to laugh at myself and from the moment I became pregnant with my first child, I proudly became a "Tiger Mom," fearless and family orientated. I wanted to love this child with the same power, devotion and care that my parents had given me.

I was orphaned as a baby and adopted at a mere eight-weeks-old. My adopted mom always said this meant I was, "loved more," as I had been "chosen" by two loving parents. They loved me unconditionally and I always felt safe, special and adored by them. When people find out that I am adopted, some look a little sad so I tell them, "It was because I was such an ugly baby that they had to give me away." This breaks the ice and gives us a laugh. But in all honesty, being adopted has done exactly what my parents wanted it to do—it made me feel loved. I wasn't had by "accident," I was "chosen" with love.

I remember once when I was a young girl and Mom was making chocolate cakes with icing. We were chatting about my birth mother. As I was licking the chocolate off the mixing spoon I asked Mom, "What do you think she looks like?"

Without skipping a beat, Mom replied, "I can only guess she would be beautiful to have had a daughter as beautiful as you." My parents' love and influence set the gold standard for parenting and I hoped that I would do the same.

## INTRODUCTION

I was driving home from hospital after giving birth to my first-born Jackson (John was driving his car behind mine) when I peered in the rear-vision mirror to see if my new sweet addition was happy in his baby seat carrier. A crystal-clear vision of three little kids sitting in a row across the back seat formed in front of my eyes. It was like a prophetic vision. I knew then and there that I would become a mother of three. And I did. We had three children in four years and life suddenly became very busy. So much for not wanting to start a family, sometimes what we think we want isn't always right.

Now, as I mentioned before, I was used to a bit of hustle. I worked in between pregnancies but had found that the practicalities of stopping and starting work again were a little too much. I began to wonder if I could work from home and look after my family. I set up a little side business (or three) selling children's toys, educational activities, clothes and books. I utilized our family home as an office and ran a party-plan style, home-based business selling kids' goods whilst raising a family.

I was essentially a one-stop-shop running three businesses that all complemented one another: children's books, toys and clothes. Genius, I know! It was empowering to make money on the side and still be actively involved in raising the family. Sure, it was busy, but I was busy anyway and thrived in the dynamic business and home-life balance that I had created. Juggling the craziness was bliss.

Around the time my first son went to preschool, my beautiful dad passed away. Having previously lost my mom, I was crippled with grief. Losing my pillars in life left a gaping hole in my heart. Life kept moving though, and I had no choice but to keep moving along with it. So I trudged through the consuming grief one day at a time, determined to hold everything together.

Next, glandular fever decided to jump into my body and slow me right down. I kept dragging myself around determined to keep up. After all, young children don't look after themselves and money doesn't spontaneously jump into your bank account. As the American activist Maya Angelou said, "Nothing works until you do." I chose not to listen to my body's signals and kept on keeping on. Over time, I ended up with four autoimmune diseases: Hashimoto's, Sjörgen's syndrome, Rheumatoid arthritis and Celiac disease. I had to carefully manage my diet, exercise and lifestyle as well as the medical treatments. Yikes! I hadn't been expecting all that.

The doctor looked at me seriously one day and asked, "How do you get up in the mornings?"

"Well," I replied, "I get one leg out of bed, then I get the other one out, and then I'm up. I have a young family you know; I have to get up." It didn't help to dwell on it.

The autoimmune diseases however did force me to slow down and assess my life. My husband had begun making some really good money in real estate, so I tried to recover and spend my time as a stay-at-home mom, volunteering at school and taking the children wherever they needed to go. I would pop into my husband's real estate firm now and then and help fill in whenever they needed some extra help. They were prospering and it was wonderful to see John's business reach new heights.

Not one to sit idle I enrolled in courses and volunteered where I could: soccer coaching, swimming secretary, helping children read—you know all the fun things! Life was great. The kids were thriving at school. John was building a successful firm and investing in real estate. I was feeling better and finally ready to look at my career whilst still managing family.

Then, like the evil villain in a movie, the Global Financial Crisis struck and spiraled the global economy out of control. The housing market collapsed in the United States and triggered a downfall across the globe, including our real-estate business and personal investments. At first, we just met the crisis head-on. Nothing lasts forever, right? Maybe we could just work harder, longer, faster—right? Wrong.

I soon discovered that it's not just finances that a GFC kills; it collapses people and destroys their livelihoods and dreams.

And that's what it did to us.

One "normal" morning at home, I went into our bedroom to chat with John. He wasn't out of bed yet and at first I couldn't see him, but when I did—it marked me forever. John was curled up and crying, his face contorted in emotional agony. I had never seen him cry before and something dropped like lead in the pit of my stomach. I knew deep down something was terribly wrong. This strong, independent and successful businessman was stripped to his core, shaking and more vulnerable than I had ever seen him. I could barely hear him as he murmured, "I just can't go back to work."

It was surreal yet I intuitively knew he just didn't mean he couldn't go back to work that day, he meant he could not go back to work: *period*. It was like an out-of-body experience for me. I could see John had had a serious breakdown and life would never be the same again. Don't ask me how I knew at the time, call it a woman's intuition, but I just knew that John was seriously ill and his mental and emotional state was not going to simply spring back.

Joining the dots backwards, I recalled that he had been a little quieter than usual lately and isolating himself from others a little more. I always knew that his soft and gentle heart didn't match the often cruel and competitive nature of real estate, though he was very good at it. A part of John shut down that day, and just as I had suspected, it was a long road back for John's mental health.

As it was all unfolding, my mind began to jump into crisis management, "What am I going to do? How will we survive? What about the kid's schooling?" My brain began planning and strategically outlining courses of action. Luckily for me, strategic planning is a strength of mine, but I had never tested it to this degree before.

As John clung to any lingering shreds of mental wellness, I had one hand on his shoulder and one part of my brain in crisis management.

> Experts in crisis management say that any crisis has three major parts:
> *Pre-crisis:* preparation and prevention
> *Crisis response:* management to respond to the crisis at hand
> *Post crisis:* preparing for future crises with good planning and strategies

Ironically, John and I did have both a "pre-crisis plan" and a "crisis response plan"—we would move house and schools and run our real estate rent-roll together until the crisis was over. But John skipped the pre-crisis preparation and went headfirst into crisis, and for this particular crisis—I was also thrust headfirst into control and management.

The economy was plunging into a recession and I had to quickly learn the ropes of my husband's business and keep him, myself and the kids above water.

I jumped into action. Within a few weeks of scrummaging around in John's real estate firm, I found out that the working culture was dismal and there were a lot of staff issues around blame and other grievances. The salespeople weren't following through and our relationships with buyers needed some nurturing and improved processes. I couldn't go to John for help, so it was sink or swim. I decided to start paddling fast.

I began to contact clients and reignite relationships. I became an overnight sales agent, studying and taking a licensed agent with me to properties to learn from, while also working on the phone much of the day, building rapport and investing in relationships. I asked the buyers thorough questions about what they wanted and really listened to their answers. I saw it as a simple "matching game"; matching clients with the houses they wanted. I sold three properties in one day, and five in the week of the main GFC crash. It was a record in the office and I had only been there four weeks.

I wasn't under any illusions though; I knew it was a recession and buyers were hunting for lower-prices and good opportunities. It was a buyer's market and they knew it, but for me it was always about the best price for a seller and to create a win-win between buyer and seller.

John and I owned property too and the GFC was impacting our financial state and with it, John's mental wellbeing. John looked at me one day and admitted honestly, "Cath, I won't get better while we have the real estate business. We have to sell." So six months down the track, we sold in a recession and lost well over a million dollars, having to sell the properties tied to the business as well.

Our family house was heavily mortgaged and our children were still at private school. It was important to me to reduce the impact on the children's lives and their education as much as possible, but I also knew that John couldn't help financially. It was up to me.

INTRODUCTION

I knew there was only one way I could go—vertical! I had to rise up and pull us out of this imploding situation. I didn't look at the facts. I didn't need a reality check: I was living the reality. I just needed to hustle beyond all definition. I needed to pull off a freakin' miracle. I didn't know if I could but I was determined to try.

I felt this could be a chance to do something that I really wanted to do. It was time to reinvent who I was. I dug deep and asked myself, *How could I make a difference, and what did I love doing?* The answer was clear: I wanted to use my passion for training, and understanding of people's behavior to help individuals become conscious, caring and successful leaders in the workplace. I saw a niche in the market for my skills and how my dream could potentially help get my family financially back on track as well.

I jumped headfirst into real estate, taking up a role in retail management, performing many different responsibilities as well as keeping up with my studies in order to start a training company. I knew every company needed great customer service and sales skills to grow their business, right? So I added to our debt and bought into a franchise because I needed to grow really quickly. I didn't have time to build from scratch. I ploughed myself into working ridiculous hours in order to grow my training business. It was tremendously hard work but I felt compelled to finally utilize my strengths and unique insights into effective leadership in business, plus I had the drive to build a long-term path out from debt for my family.

I'll never forget meeting with my first potential client. It was a well-known company with 300 staff and they had advertised for "Team Sales Training." I was excited because I knew I was the person to deliver it. I dressed in my best power suit and matching briefcase before purposefully setting off to meet with the manager. It was a 50km (31 miles) drive so John generously offered to drive me.

The manager in charge of recruiting a sales trainer was a nice guy and we chatted easily; about halfway through our conversation though, he secretly confessed that he wanted to leave his job and work for me. It disrupted the natural flow of the meeting and red flags popped up in my brain. It became increasingly obvious that this manager was really seeking to advance his own career, rather than train his staff. It seemed the advertising was perhaps more of a recruitment strategy for himself, which would later prove to be true.

Afterwards, I slumped back into the car dejectedly and John asked, "What happened?"

I didn't want to talk about it but John sensed my obvious disillusionment and suggested we have a coffee in a nearby shopping center.

As I was consoling myself with a good dose of caffeine, I looked over and noticed a travel agency business, Harvey World Travel. A little spark kindled in my mind. I had heard that travel agencies did a lot of staff training. As I was already dressed and ready to go I took the plunge, telling John I'd be back in a minute.

I felt nervous but determined as I introduced myself to a staff member drawing on all my years of experience to appear open, confident and friendly. The travel agent was very receptive to my introduction and replied that the manager had in fact been talking about staff training recently for multiple stores. She was happy to get the manager to talk with me. Could my luck be turning?

The manager appeared and we instantly hit it off. She was interested in my background in leadership and management and wanted to know all about our company's training style and some of the more subtle "soft skills" training we offered such as body language and language sales patterns. I felt a moment of uncertainty when she admitted that she had already spoken to a couple of training companies and wasn't sure which way she wanted to go. Then she smiled, "But I think I want to go with you!"

I was fist-pumping and somersaulting on the inside. My smile to her said it all.

Next she surprised me by doing something few people do in a first meeting: she gave me some other contacts. Businesses she knew whom also required staff training. What a hot ticket! I phoned every single contact that same day and over time, one lead led to another.

My first training package was $3000 per person and I started with 30 people. By the end of that year, with some good old-fashioned caring for people skills, my company had hit one million dollars in contracts for our training. Over the coming years, we expanded to 18 staff on the Sunshine Coast as well as working with 36 contract trainers Australia-wide. This successful period became the miracle I'd been looking for, or should I say—became the miracle I had been working all those long hours for.

When I finally saw the annual figures and realized my family was no longer in that hole of debt, a strange wave of relief and exhaustion coursed through my body. That year was in some ways a blur and in other ways, forever etched in my memory; a strange but true paradox.

Originally, all I had aimed to do was recover our lost money, yet now I was reporting to our accountant with "new money." I must admit, it does seem ironic when you think about it: to have lost one million dollars and made one million dollars all in the same year! I cried with relief, although it wasn't over, we were out of financial ruin—or so I thought.

Our accountant calculated we had to pay nearly $400,000 in tax! I nearly cried for a second time for very different reasons. *How could this be?* I had worked so hard to get us out of this crisis and now I was being thrown back into additional debt. We had sold all our investments at a loss! It didn't seem fair.

I had to leave my children every day, only making it home for dinner, and what for? For this kick in the guts! It felt like a brutal punch pelted full force into my chest.

Despite my disillusionment I did know one thing—something I was doing was working. I had learned how to make money fast and how to deliver transformative education and training. I had learned how to build teams and provide them with life-affirming strategies. I had learned how to manage teams and build leaders.

So, once again, I put my skills to work with the burning desire to get out of debt and into prosperity. By then however, I had gained so much more than just aiming to lift a financial burden; I had fast-tracked my learning about leadership and what worked and what didn't. I felt like I had taken an accelerated crash-course and the whole crazy journey was beginning to make sense.

Working at this accelerated rate, gave me access to top CEOs and leaders. It put me in the trenches with their employees and showed me what was really happening in business. One of the most important things I discovered was that the leaders who were more conscious of their people, and took the time to learn about themselves, achieved better results. I learned that when leaders understood the behaviors and leadership style of their team, then a good sturdy culture could be forged and success was inevitable.

I also saw first-hand, the devastating consequences of a poor hiring decision. The thousands of dollars wasted on employees who weren't a right fit for the job. It wasn't that they were bad or ill-equipped team members; it was because they weren't "matched" for the right job. Often, companies hire from a well-crafted resume rather than addressing the natural leadership style, behaviors and soft skills of an individual (more on that in the following chapters). All these big and little things added up and revealed the strengths and weaknesses at large.

Witnessing so many positive outcomes from teaching conscious leadership skills, allowed me to see the enormous consequences of those businesses and leaders not doing it, not being aware, not being conscious to others and their needs. The results of remaining unconscious were catastrophic to some businesses and they never returned to their former glory. Think about companies like Kodak, Xerox or Yahoo who remained unconscious to innovation and the natural evolution within their own industries and paid the ultimate price.

These lessons and experiences accumulated over many years allowed me to build a business, an awesome business that put me on the road back to recovery, and then past it. I had the pleasure of helping thousands of people and countless businesses. I became wonderfully successful and even wrote a book in 2017 about the importance of first impressions in business called *The Million Dollar Handshake* published by Hachette Australia.[1]

The book was bought by four global publishers, reproduced in numerous languages and Seven Dials Orion Books in the UK made it their "Business Book of the Year." It also gave me an international platform for more speaking gigs. I presented to groups in China, India, Australia, New Zealand, Singapore, Hong Kong, UAE, Saudi Arabia and the UK to name a few. It was incredible to be impacting others, providing them with tried-and-tested tools in order to grow themselves and their businesses.

Yes, I was rejoicing again: and very thankful for every sweet breath of success. But it wasn't the prosperity that anchored me to this work; it's always been passion and purpose. I truly love what I do and doing it every day is an absolute blessing.

I became inspired to give back more and devoted a lot of my extra time to the charities I had long supported. Giving back was always an absolute must for me, even during our toughest times, but it was now wonderful to give more. I'm dedicated to so many incredible charities that do life-altering work.

When I began my own business, I said to my husband, "Ten percent must go to charity!" As the business grew, I started to help raise funds for orphans, visit orphanages in Uganda and help build houses. The book *The Million Dollar Handshake* became a tool to help fundraise and one-third of all profits go to charity.

This book, *The Conscious Leader* will be supporting The Bombay Mothers And Children's Welfare Society helping disadvantaged children and families receive treatment for cancer.[2]

I'll never forget when working in Calcutta I saw the sign at Mother Teresa's home—*If you can't feed 100, feed one*—and I know that each of you reading this, can all feed one and make a difference.

## IGNITING THE CONSCIOUS LEADER WITHIN

In 2018, we made the big decision to sell our family home of 29 years (the one I had fought so hard to keep) and we bought 17 acres just 15 minutes from some of the most beautiful beaches in the world. I wanted some property to come home to after all my long-haul flights working in cities around the world. I longed for space and fresh air, a country home for all the family whenever anyone needed to recharge and where we could be self-sufficient, growing food if there happened to be a world crisis in the future.

Unfortunately as I finish writing this book, COVID-19 has spread throughout the world. A check recently arrived in the mail made out to me for $9,500 for a keynote talk. I had to return it to them as travel restrictions had tightened and my livelihood was on hold, all conferences canceled. John jokes about people paying me to speak, "I'd pay you not to!" Yes, even after 29 years together, I know he still loves me.

But as life would have it, and all jokes aside, I find myself in another great challenge. But this one isn't like the GFC. I am aware that operating on fear is only a short-term strategy. Once again, almost overnight, my business of speaking to groups and running group-based workshops and events has been derailed by external forces.

But I now know it's how I respond to it that makes all the difference. I can't change this new crisis, but I can adapt and reinvent myself or my business direction. I can learn new skills and roll with the changes rather than resist them. I've been through an external crisis before with the GFC, and I learned that the key to overcoming it was in my internal response.

Through the peaks and troughs of life, it's important to remember, "Life happens." That sometimes no matter how hard you try or how watertight your business strategy is—shit happens that you can't control. As the great Holocaust survivor Viktor Frankl taught us, "When we are no longer able to change a situation, we are challenged to change ourselves."[3]

I agree.

Your crisis may be a global one, like the GFC or COVID-19, or it may be a domestic one from within your own household, maybe an illness, job loss or death. The scale of the crisis isn't the most important factor. The most important factor is to wake up and become conscious of your options. Become aware of what you can control and how you can ignite transformation within yourself and the lives of others.

Finishing this book is a direct result of that internal ignition switch. This book isn't just a business idea; it's a spiritual emergence of something deep within me. These messages and principles come from a deep place within and begged to come out and be shared with the world.

I offer you, *The Conscious Leader: how to lead a life worth living through crises and beyond*. A book that stirred from my soul and lifetime of experiences and poured itself onto the pages with a relentless urgency. The principles in this book really stand as the cornerstone of my working life and provide a platform from which anyone can use and soar to great heights. I truly love to see and support greatness in others.

We must however remain conscious in knowing that *conscious leadership* isn't only about leading when times are all wonderful and prosperous; a truly conscious leader steps up when crises hit and responds to the situation with purposeful awareness.

A conscious leader doesn't look for someone to blame and shame but looks to the future and creates a new type of leadership based on humanity's deepest needs. The great secret is: you can be that leader today. Be *The Conscious Leader*.

The intention of this book is to decode the art of consciousness in order to empower situational leaders and leaders in life with the skills to make more intentional and purpose-driven decisions that create better outcomes for yourself, for the business, for communities and for the planet.

Welcome to the decade of *The Conscious Leader*.

## CHAPTER 1

# LEADING YOURSELF

### WHAT TYPE OF LEADER ARE YOU? THE CHOICE IS YOURS

*"Self leadership dominos from three main sources: our knowledge, our behavior, our emotion."*
**Catherine Molloy**

What are your first thoughts when you wake up in the morning? What am I doing today? What will I wear? What shall I have for breakfast, Coco Pops or muesli? Or perhaps; where do I need to go? How will I get there?

From the time you wake, you are making decisions that will lead your life for the day, and you keep making countless decisions every hour. Some will be bigger than others such as how you respond to situations and how you react to others while some will be more subtle like your emotion-based decisions. You are constantly making decisions and *leading* yourself until you fall asleep again for the night.

Research from Microsoft[1] tells us that we make over 35,000 decisions a day; Cornwell University suggests we make 226.7 decisions each day about food alone.[2] And that's just food! If you're in business, you make thousands of decisions each day and let's be honest—every one of them matters!

The dictionary defines the word "decision" as the act or need to make up our minds through a process of elimination; this implies when we do decide on a direction to take, we "cut off" other directions. This sounds limiting doesn't it?

On the other hand, the word "choice" means the power, the opportunity or the right to choose. It is about our mindset as we consider all the facts. Choice comes from the concept "to perceive" meaning we choose what we believe is right or wrong based on the perceived consequences for ourselves. And, as we become more conscious leaders, how those consequences affect others.

There is a fine line between decision-making and choosing; cutting off options versus choosing pathways for ourselves, our families or our teams. It's a very powerful reality to operate from.

Everyone has their own motives and methods for making the decisions and choices that lead their actions. Some people lead themselves by doing exactly what they want to their own end. Others want to lead by setting examples for their family, colleagues, sporting teammates and perhaps even their friends. No matter how we do it, all the decisions and choices we make in our lives are aimed at *leading ourselves to an outcome*.

We lead ourselves to outcomes every day but we don't always lead positively or lead consciously. We have a choice in every moment. When we become more aware of our leadership style, the characteristics of the people we're leading, the peculiarities of the situation we are in and what we need to achieve for the greatest good, we can change our outcomes for the better. In other words, becoming *more conscious* leads to better outcomes.

> *"Leading yourself well is a conscious choice."*
> **Catherine Molloy**

Being a conscious leader is a choice. It's not just something you fall into by accident. It's a skill you develop over time. Just as becoming a great pianist begins by learning all the keys consciously and hitting a few wrong notes along the way, leadership develops through being conscious and learning through experience and effort. The act of being conscious every day eventually leads to self-mastery.

So what does it mean to be conscious? The dictionary has numerous definitions that all describe an inner awareness:
- *Aware of one's own existence, sensations, thoughts and surroundings.*
- *Fully aware of or sensitive to something*
- *Having the mental faculties fully active*
- *Known to oneself*
- *Aware of what one is doing*

The famous psychoanalyst Carl Gustav Jung said, "One does not become enlightened by imagining figures of light but by making the darkness conscious."[3]

That's exactly what many conscious leaders do—they pull beliefs and perceptions out of the darkness, into the light and make them conscious. Nelson Mandela did this when he brought the injustice of apartheid to the world's attention. His conscientious leadership style was so emotive and compelling to both sides that his efforts unified a country that had been racially divided for over forty years. The prejudice of apartheid wasn't pretty for everyone to look at and become fully aware of, but it was vital that they did so. Nothing would have changed if such inequality remained in the shadows of so-called social acceptance.

Being a conscious leader is the entire premise of this book. Its fierce intent is to develop more conscious leaders over the globe and change our world for the better. This book is about bringing new and emerging leaders into the light of self-reflection and understanding to develop their skills even further in a fast-changing world. After all, it's our leaders that we look to in times of crises.

Now of course, being a leading-edge and conscious leader is not all rainbows and lollipops. It's not always easy. Being a conscious leader means getting real about things, becoming aware of the consequences of your actions (or inactions) and doing what is right more than doing what is popular. Conscious leaders are not self-serving; they serve humanity. **They are self-reflective and yet socially active and courageous.**

One thing that I have noticed more than anything is that conscious leaders deliberately and consistently work on becoming more aware. They don't leave it to chance or imagine that a sudden bolt of lightning will strike them down with newfound knowledge. They investigate global and local matters themselves, with a natural curiosity. They aim to be better and do better every day.

They want to know what helps, what harms, what hinders and what will happen if they choose one course of action over another. They aren't the type to sweep things under the rug and turn a blind eye. In fact, they will flip the rug over and have a darn good look underneath. Conscious leaders are optimistic about humanity, and yet not blinded to see when we are in crisis.

## GOOD SELF-LEADERSHIP COMES FIRST

The truth is, you need to consciously lead yourself well before you can successfully lead others. As the Dalai Lama said, "To be aware of a single shortcoming in oneself is more useful than to be aware of a thousand in someone else."[4]

So what exactly is self-leadership?

In many ways, it's simply a modern term for an age-old concept around self-awareness and acting within your values.

Charles Manz, who first used the term in 1983, defined "self-leadership" as "A comprehensive self-influence perspective that concerns leading oneself."[5] While leadership experts Bryant and Kazan defined self-leadership as, "The practice of intentionally influencing your thinking, feeling and actions towards your objective/s."[6]

Taking these terms into account and through my experiences I have developed my own definition for effective self-leadership: **Consciously leading your thoughts, your emotions, your decisions, your behaviors and your relationships using positive and purposeful choices.**

It's good to remember the most important person you need to influence each day is yourself. That is the first step to becoming a leader worth following. As the ancient Chinese philosopher Lao Tzu put it, "Mastering yourself is true power."

## ARE YOU A LEADER WORTH FOLLOWING?

Take a look in the mirror and ask yourself: *What sort of leader am I? What sort of leader do I want to be for others?*

I want you to bring your unconscious behaviors into the light and make them conscious, even if it's a bit uncomfortable at first. If you're having a rough morning and already running late, do you arrive to work smiling or grumpy? Whichever answer you choose; I want you to know that your actions when you walk into work (or anywhere for that matter) is a choice.

Now think about the consequences of that choice. Imagine how others will respond to a smile or a grump. The choice you make, to smile or be grumpy, will either motivate or dampen those spirits around you. Of course, you can seize the moment and decide to stop being grumpy too. This is a simple yet game-changing decision you can make in order to lead yourself better. Sounds simple right?

Now ask yourself: *Am I a leader worth following?* Or are you just going through the motions? Are you confident you know your own leadership style and the values you hold, or are you just guessing?

The way you lead yourself might change from day to day due to subliminal factors (such as physical well-being or external events). I want you to become conscious of those factors and how they affect you—will you smile or be grumpy? Becoming conscious of your relationship to each moment, each situation, each person (including yourself and your moods) is ground-breaking and allows you to consciously choose your leadership style.

## SEEING THE SHADOW IN GREATNESS

Back in 2018, I was working with a top CEO in the airline industry; let's call him Tony. The team identified Tony as a strong leader in many ways but they also said that he wasn't a great listener. Now, Tony knew the theory on listening. He had read all the leadership books and was well versed in the importance of being an active listener. The problem was just that. Tony knew how important listening was but he just didn't practice it. After hearing some of the feedback about his poor listening skills, Tony recognized he had to change.

We used role-playing techniques with Tony to help identify why people felt they weren't being listened to and to help him consciously activate his listening skills. We also utilized role-playing tools to show him how to be engaged, patient and ask questions to gain an understanding of a situation. Tony added these additional listening skills to his own leadership style and the result was immediately positive. His team felt valued, as he was taking them seriously and the entire work culture instantly transformed. It was phenomenal.

Although Tony had many incredible leadership skills prior to our workshop, he neglected the one that everyone needed, his shadow side. When he finally practiced new active listening skills, the entire team transformed. It was this essential ingredient that made all the difference between Tony being a good leader and becoming a great leader.

Tony's lesson highlights three important points to remember if you want to become a great leader:
- Be open to feedback
- Seek out a mentor or a professional coach when needed
- Add skills to your own style to make you a leader people will listen to and respect.

## HOW ARE YOU LEADING RIGHT NOW?

It's critical to become open to your own style and see where you can enhance it. Just like Tony, sometimes we don't see our own blind spots. I often use a multiple-choice diagnostic tool called DISC with my clients and team to assess leadership styles. It provides a snapshot of how people are likely to behave as a leader today, perhaps even subconsciously.

Take a minute to decide where you are right at this moment in your life and career. Are you where you'd like to be? Remember that the answer does not define you; it just helps you acknowledge where you're at so you can adapt and learn and strengthen the way you lead in the future.

## LET'S GET REAL

To begin to understand your own leadership behaviors I have a quick mini-quiz for you to analyze which skills you feel you have and which skills you would like to improve on in order to become the leader you want to be.

# WHICH STYLE OF LEADER ARE YOU?

Choose the statement that best describes you.

| If you are: | If you are: |
|---|---|
| fast-paced, talk loudly at times, love reaching and setting goals, taking action and making THINGS happen, choose **Option A**. | reserved when meeting people for the first time, like to take time to think about your answers, work through your tasks diligently, choose **Option B**. |

**OPTION A**  **OPTION B**

If you chose **Option A**, now choose which leadership style you identify with the most:

| I focus on principles, goals and tasks. | I like to energize/ engage team members. |
|---|---|
| ✓ I make quick decisions.<br>✓ I like systems and use processes when setting goals.<br>✓ I like making lists and using lists to get my work done. | ✓ I am loud and have charisma.<br>✓ I like to be flexible and respond to the moment.<br>✓ If I make a list, I usually lose it. |

**DIRECTING**  **INFLUENCING**
**(TASK ORIENTED)**  **(PEOPLE ORIENTED)**

If you chose **Option B**, now choose which leadership style you identify with the most:

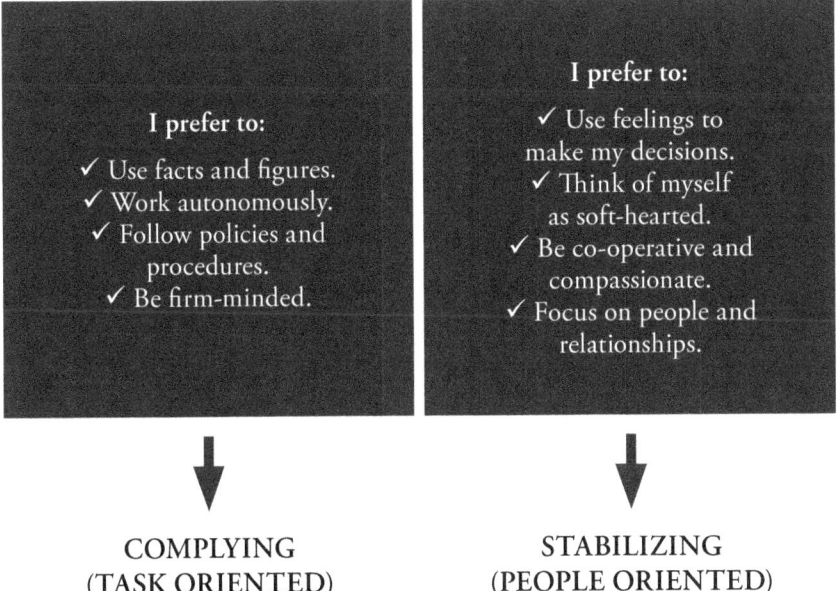

COMPLYING
(TASK ORIENTED)

STABILIZING
(PEOPLE ORIENTED)

Now that you have chosen your preferred leadership style, match your style to a bird symbol in the following pages to confirm your strengths in this leadership style.

# SO WHAT SYMBOL ARE YOU AND HOW ARE YOU LIKELY TO LEAD?

**DIRECTING**
- Vision
- Goals
- Demanding
- Innovative
- Resolute

**The Eagle:** Looks at the eagle-view of a situation, the visionary. Sets high goals and expects them to be met. Innovative and often demanding in nature, the Eagle flies above details and is goal, task and action oriented.

**INFLUENCING**
- Equality
- Action
- Variety
- Pioneering
- Energising

**The Peacock:** The Peacock is a social creature with a high degree of influence and charisma. The Peacock cares about people and what people think. Energetic by nature, the Peacock thrives in a dynamic and changing environment.

## STABILIZING
- Calm/Humble
- Steady
- Harmonious
- Legacy
- Inclusive

**The Dove:** Calm and stable by nature, the Dove is a harmonious and caring creature who thrives in an inclusive and nurturing environment. The Dove is often a symbol of peace and kindness who focuses on people and relationships.

## COMPLYING
- Structure
- Responsible
- Overseer
- Deliberate
- Conscientious

**The Owl:** Conscientious and responsible, the Owl is a dedicated soul who focuses on policies and procedures with great detail. The Owl enjoys working autonomously and is a natural at handling and assessing facts and figures.

My leadership style is

## STRENGTHS AND WEAKNESSES

Every person has both strengths and weaknesses. Some people in the corporate world refer to them as balconies and basements. For example, if you're standing on the balcony, you are soaring high in your strengths while if you're in the basement you are working to the negative aspects of your strengths. For example, an Eagle (Directing style) is a natural visionary, however in the basement the Eagle may appear as a leader who says, "It's my way or the highway!"

As a Gallup-Certified Strengths Coach,[7] I like to remind people that strengths and weaknesses are part of being human. No one arrives in the world with superhero strengths and no weaknesses.

Our basements (weaknesses) aren't necessarily a problem if we become aware of them. It's when we are unconscious to them that they wreak havoc. And when we are unconscious of how the other styles perceive our strengths is when our strengths can become our weaknesses too. Let me give you an example.

I once worked with a top female CEO, Sophie, who was on the cusp of burnout. She came to me under the proviso that she was getting coached to become a stronger leader. However, I soon realized, she didn't need to be "stronger," she needed to be more relatable and vulnerable. You see, Sophie had made it to the top of her predominately male-dominated industry and had built up a lot of strength, resilience and determination traits that had helped her get to the top.

But she was afraid to show empathy or build a relationship with her team in case it was perceived as "weak." Sophie had spent so long building up her hard-earned skills and strengths that she ignored some of the most essential soft skills. She was over-working her strengths to compensate and was on the road to burnout.

Sophie and I had to re-evaluate the true meaning of strengths and weaknesses and though it took a lot of coaching, I had to assure her that consciously showing her true self was in fact a great act of courage and strength.

My point here is to withhold judgment, to not critique yourself harshly but to instead be open and curious to your style. Don't make quick assessments of what you believe is a weakness because once you are aware of it, you are in control. And that's what this book is all about—being conscious and aware of yourself and others.

> *"The key to growth is the introduction of higher dimensions of consciousness into our awareness."*
> **Lao Tzu**

Which of the following styles, strengths and weaknesses do you identify with?

## DIRECTING (AUTOCRATIC)

**BALCONY**

*The Visionary*

- Vision
- Goals
- Innovative
- Resolute
- Pioneering
- Delegating
- Makes quick decisions

**BASEMENT**

*My Way Or The Highway*

- Doesn't include others in making decisions
- No details
- Wants status
- I am boss, you follow
- Demanding

# INFLUENCING (DEMOCRATIC)

**BALCONY**

*The Charismatic*

- Equality
- Fun
- Active
- Variety
- Pioneering
- Energizing
- Listen to others' opinions
- Allows creative thinking
- Decisions made with input of others
- Gives employees a sense of purpose

**BASEMENT**

*Ticking time bomb*

- *Everything's okay, everything's okay… boom! No, it's not and there is an explosion…*
- Lacks follow through
- Lacks researching facts
- Trouble having difficult conversations

# STABILIZING (LAISSEZ-FAIRE)

## BALCONY

*The Servant*

- Calm
- Steady
- Harmonious
- Legacy
- Inclusive
- Helpful
- Humble
- Decision making left to groups
- Does not criticize

## BASEMENT

*The Hanger*

- Hanging loose, hanging tough, hanging in there
- No idea what is really happening
- Slow to adapt to change
- Won't confront others
- Little or no control of situations
- Provides little or no direction

## COMPLYING (BUREAUCRATIC)

### BALCONY
*The Logical*
- Structured
- Responsible
- Overseer
- Resolute
- Deliberate
- Listens and considers

### BASEMENT
*Baffle With Bullshit Rules*
- Makes others follow the rules and if they don't, they create another rule!
- Doesn't compromise
- Doesn't delegate
- Doesn't make quick decisions
- Resistant to change
- Lack of freedom for workers
- Disencourages innovation

---

**Take the Bonus Behavioral Style Quiz**

On completion, you will be able to download your responses to a PDF. Responses can also be sent directly to Catherine via the interactive book at deanpublishing.com/consciousleader.

In the following table, identify your leadership style (Directing, Influencing, Stabilizing or Complying). Write in the traits you have at this particular snapshot in time. Don't forget to list balconies as well as basements, you may want to fill in a few sections for these.

What's your preferred style?

☐ D   ☐ I   ☐ S   ☐ C

What are your strengths (balconies) and weaknesses (basements)?

| Strengths/Balconies | Weaknesses/Basements |
|---|---|
| | |
| | |
| | |

### DIRECTING

Balcony:
The visionary

Basement:
My way or the highway

### INFLUENCING

Balcony:
The charismatic

Basement:
Ticking time bomb

### COMPLYING

Balcony:
The logical

Basement:
Baffle with bullshit rules

### STABILIZING

Balcony:
The servant

Basement:
The hanger

## COMMON LEADERSHIP STYLES

Now that we have identified some of our strengths (balconies) and weaknesses (basements)—we can also look at some common leadership styles. You may identify with some traits or skills that you possess or some you would like to aspire to. You may even discover that you sit in the "basement" of some of these too.

It can be important to identify strengths you may want to add to your leadership toolkit and acknowledge some of the basement descriptions you currently identify with. This can help you eliminate these behaviors from your leadership toolkit. What you remove is equally important as what you may add.

For example, the first common leadership style is—visionary. You may choose to create clear visions and directions (balcony), however you may also identify that in the past you lacked the discipline to implement them (basement). The key to balancing this is obviously more about eradicating your basement behavior than only increasing your strengths.

After you have looked at these common leadership styles and identified with some of them, ask yourself how you feel about it. Is there anything you relate to or aspire to? Do you possess many of these qualities?

Now, identify which style of DISC style (bird) you believe each leadership style is. Place a tick in the box: D, I, S, or C:

- D for Directing
- I for Influencing
- S for Stabilizing
- C for Complying

You may find one or two DISC styles stand out, or perhaps it's all four. But it is worth analyzing in order to understanding the leadership style you want, or work with in the future. This will help you create win-win solutions and understand others from their own leadership style.

## THE VISIONARY

Where the leader sees potential for how the future should look and then takes steps to get there. Is driven by the long-term future, by what a company can become. Is naturally perceptive and has an uncanny sense of the hidden, the unspoken, the unknown.

| STRENGTHS | WEAKNESSES |
|---|---|
| • Creates a clear vision and direction<br>• Motivates and inspires team members to go forward<br>• Openly shares information<br>• Determined<br>• Works towards achieving goals set | • Could result in too much risk taking<br>• Team members not sharing vision<br>• Lack of clarity of vision<br>• Visionary Leaders often retain control because they believe in themselves so much, leaving organizations without successors<br>• Failure to implement vision could demotivate team members |

☐ D  ☐ I  ☐ S  ☐ C

## THE CHARISMATIC

This leader relies on their charm, positive personality, and the success of their projects is closely linked to how they feel about themselves. This is an innovative, thinking-outside-of-the-box kind of leader. He/she works co-operatively with the whole, sharing ideas to improve and develop innovative solutions to problems for the company.

| STRENGTHS | WEAKNESSES |
| --- | --- |
| • Equality<br>• Fun<br>• Active<br>• Variety<br>• Pioneering<br>• Energizing<br>• Listens to others' opinions<br>• Allows creative thinking<br>• Day-to-day decisions made with input from others<br>• Gives employees a sense of purpose<br>• Uses guidance as suggestion<br>• Inspires and motivates | • Success of projects and initiatives are closely linked to their presence<br>• Confidence of a team drops when the leader isn't present<br>• They are not great with follow up<br>• No clear direction at times<br>• Trouble having difficult conversations<br>• Motivation drops |

☐ D  ☐ I  ☐ S  ☐ C

## THE SERVANT/SUPPORTIVE

This leader prefers power sharing within the group, prioritizing the needs of the team and encouraging collective decision making. They delegate and assign tasks to employees but also provide the skills needed to complete tasks. Rather than solely focusing on making the organization thrive, its main goal really is to serve. Its primary objective is the growth and well-being of its people. Instead of having all the power, this leader shares the power and supports people's need to develop and perform at their best.

| STRENGTHS | WEAKNESSES |
|---|---|
| • Improves diversity<br>• Boosts morale<br>• Will work with team member to complete task<br>• Encourages team work<br>• Focuses on relationships<br>• Builds trust<br>• Active listener<br>• Sharing leader<br>• Shows empathy | • Lack of authority<br>• Places team above tasks so doesn't always meet business objectives<br>• Slow to make decisions<br>• Resists change<br>• Not adhering to schedules and time restraints<br>• Lack of future planning |

☐ D ☐ I ☐ S ☐ C

## THE LOGICAL

This leader loves facts and figures and is grounded in evidence-based principles for guaranteed results. Often attentive to details, factual and always clear, the Logical Leader communicates ideas precisely and effectively. The ultimate goal is to arrive at the truth of things. Problem solving for this leader involves structure, relationships of facts and reasoning based on reliable sources.

| STRENGTHS | WEAKNESSES |
|---|---|
| • Structure<br>• Responsible<br>• Overseer<br>• Resolute<br>• Deliberate<br>• Listens and considers<br>• Gets facts straight<br>• Seeks to arrive at the truth of things<br>• Mindful of the origin of ideas | • Inhibits creative ideas<br>• Doesn't enjoy small talk which isolates some team members<br>• Gets stuck in thinking<br>• Overanalyzes situations and people<br>• Fear of being wrong<br>• Doesn't always see the big picture<br>• Goals may not be achieved |

☐ D    ☐ I    ☐ S    ☐ C

## THE AUTHENTIC

This leader is self-aware, they understand their strengths and limitations. The Authentic Leader is built on character not style. They are transparent and understand they make mistakes. They can become rigid in being true to their ideals. They may also be a good coach and mentor while retaining their authenticity.

| STRENGTHS | WEAKNESSES |
| --- | --- |
| • Self-aware<br>• They promote positive psychological wellbeing<br>• Encourages self-esteem<br>• Empowers followers<br>• Increase performance<br>• Reduce burnout<br>• Enabler<br>• Trusting<br>• Ethical<br>• Leads with heart | • If values don't match, this leader won't be accepted<br>• They want to do the right thing but who decides what the right thing is?<br>• Locked into rigid views of their leadership style<br>• Can appear rude and insensitive<br>• Refusing to change<br>• Not adapting to a different style to meet the situation |

☐ D  ☐ I  ☐ S  ☐ C

## THE AUTHORITARIAN/AUTOCRATIC

Where the leader of a team makes decisions without input from team members. Has full control of the team/organization. The Authoritarian Leader dictates policies and procedures, solely deciding on what goals and paths the organization will be taking. Directs and controls all activities with no significant participation from other members and subordinates on the team.

| STRENGTHS | WEAKNESSES |
| --- | --- |
| • Strong control over team<br>• Control centralized<br>• Retention of power<br>• Decisions made quickly<br>• Constructive criticism | • Employee resentment about the way decisions are made<br>• Lack of activity when boss is unavailable<br>• Limited creativity and innovation<br>• One-way communication, from top-down<br>• Creates a sense of fear<br>• Rarely considers team suggestions<br>• Low group morale |

☐ D   ☐ I   ☐ S   ☐ C

## THE DEMOCRATIC/PARTICIPATIVE

This leader allows all members of a team to participate in decision-making. Democratic leadership is one of the most effective leadership styles. The leader makes decisions based on the input of each team member. Although he or she makes the final call, each employee has an equal say on a project's direction. This leadership style has been found as one of the most effective with higher productivity and the feeling of being valued in the work place.

| STRENGTHS | WEAKNESSES |
|---|---|
| • Empowers team members<br>• Distributes responsibility<br>• Team members directed through guidance and suggestions<br>• Creates team member satisfaction<br>• Encourages innovation<br>• Embraces flexibility and adaption<br>• Two-way communication<br>• High levels of job satisfaction | • Time consuming, can be slower than normal to make decisions<br>• Reduction in efficiency<br>• Difficulties in accountability<br>• Need experienced/skilled team members to work well<br>• Less control maintained |

☐ D   ☐ I   ☐ S   ☐ C

## THE LAISSEZ-FAIRE/FREE REIN

Where the leader has a hands-off approach and allows the team to make decisions. From its literal translation from the French, "let them do," this kind of leadership allows just that. This is the least intrusive amongst the different kinds of leadership. The leader puts full trust into the employees' ability and capacity. This works well when the team is highly skilled, experienced and educated.

| STRENGTHS | WEAKNESSES |
|---|---|
| • Empowers team members to take control of decision-making<br>• Boosts productivity<br>• Encourages innovation and creativity<br>• Creates pride in work<br>• Lets team get on with tasks at hand | • Little or no control<br>• Lack of group cohesion<br>• Leader isn't leading<br>• Downplays role of leader<br>• Lack of guidance/direction to team members<br>• Limits staff development<br>• May overlook growth opportunities<br>• Lack of regular feedback<br>• Creates chaos |

☐ D  ☐ I  ☐ S  ☐ C

## THE BUREAUCRAT

Where leaders focus their attention on the rules, policies and practices of the organization. One of the most common forms of management. The Bureaucrat goes by the book. Follows fixed official duties and adheres to a system of rules. Listening and consideration of ideas from employees are heard but more often than not are rejected if they contradict the organization's policies. This leadership style is implemented in highly regulated environments.

| STRENGTHS | WEAKNESSES |
| --- | --- |
| • Consistency<br>• Job security<br>• Direction<br>• Centralized power<br>• Predictability | • No innovation<br>• Low team member morale<br>• Difficulties performing or changing due to red tape<br>• Can create boredom in team members<br>• Rejects employees' input |

☐ D   ☐ I   ☐ S   ☐ C

## THE HUB AND SPOKE

This is a leader who needs to be in control of almost everything. Information and decisions are made solely by this leader—"The Hub." The spokes are the employees, all moving/functioning as defined by the hub. This kind of leader believes no one can do things better than they can.

| STRENGTHS | WEAKNESSES |
|---|---|
| • Commanding of themselves and others<br>• Resolute<br>• Pioneering<br>• Decisive<br>• In control | • Overly strong<br>• Motivated by coercion<br>• Directs by using commands<br>• Micromanages<br>• Keeps everyone separate<br>• Controls everything<br>• "If it's to be done right, I need to do it!" |

☐ D  ☐ I  ☐ S  ☐ C

## THE COACH

Where leaders focus on identifying and nurturing skills in teams and individuals required to achieve team goals. The Coach often focuses on identifying the strengths of every individual in his team and from there, nurtures and helps them develop as individuals, for the benefit of the team. They often create good strategies to work from so the team can function better.

| STRENGTHS | WEAKNESSES |
| --- | --- |
| • Connects team skills to organizational goals<br>• Improves individual performances by cross-skilling<br>• Increases skills in the whole team<br>• Increases overall team motivation and performance<br>• Creates loyalty<br>• Builds strong teams | • Perceived favoritism within the team<br>• Can coach at unplanned times which creates unplanned outcomes, or no outcomes at all<br>• Can pass on bad habits to team members<br>• May coach in areas that they don't have skills in |

☐ D   ☐ I   ☐ S   ☐ C

## THE STRATEGIST

Where the leader thinks, acts and influences others in ways that promotes success in the organization. This leader has strategic vision for the team and helps in motivating and pushing others to gain that same vision for the benefit of the organization. It is a desirable leadership trait in many companies because its way of thinking can support multiple types of employees at once.

| STRENGTHS | WEAKNESSES |
| --- | --- |
| • Encourages objective thinking<br>• Ensures success of an organization<br>• Reduces resistance to change<br>• Promotes collaboration and unity<br>• Develops new visions and directions<br>• Effectively manages resources<br>• Sustains organizational culture | • Unsure of the best direction for the company (if everyone else has input)<br>• Time consuming behavior<br>• Needs a skillful leader to implement strategies<br>• Could result in failure due to too much risk taking<br>• Prone to overstaffing |

☐ D    ☐ I    ☐ S    ☐ C

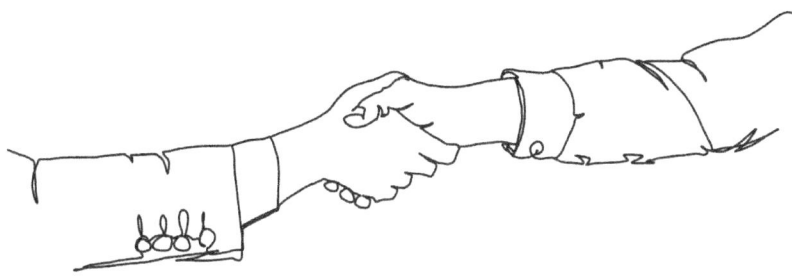

## THE TRANSACTIONALIST

Where leaders promote team member compliance through both reward and punishment. Transactional Leaders establish a clear chain of command and help establish roles and responsibilities for each employee. They reward employees based on what they do. They use a carrot and stick approach in their reward system to encourage or discourage employees.

| STRENGTHS | WEAKNESSES |
|---|---|
| • Values order and structure<br>• Works well with motivated team members<br>• Uses influence to inspire<br>• High-performing<br>• Works well in crisis situations focusing on achieving a task<br>• Clear chain of command<br>• Offers exchange and reward for good performance | • Reduces individuality in the organization<br>• Limits innovation and creativity<br>• Focuses on consequences rather than rewards<br>• Can result in bare minimum work if goals are easily obtained or unrealistic<br>• Employees unlikely to reach their full creative potential |

☐ D  ☐ I  ☐ S  ☐ C

## THE TRANSFORMATIONAL

Where the leader is always trying to transform and improve conventions through motivation. Constantly pushing employees outside their comfort zones with the goal of improving, inspiring and transforming them for the benefit of the organization. The Transformational Leader is a growth-minded leader who persistently motivates employees to reach their potentials and see what they are capable of. These leaders may require a more detailed team to successfully implement their visions.

| STRENGTHS | WEAKNESSES |
| --- | --- |
| • High expectations<br>• Effectively communicates<br>• Inspires team members to reach goals<br>• Builds trust and enthusiasm<br>• Sets targets in place<br>• Visionary<br>• Motivates employees to see what they are capable of | • Team members burnout<br>• Goals not reached due to being unrealistic<br>• Details not paid attention to<br>• Pushes employees too often out of their comfort zone<br>• Loses sight of team members learning curves<br>• Often changes the goal posts |

☐ D  ☐ I  ☐ S  ☐ C

## THE PACESETTER

Where leaders have a strong urge to succeed and set high standards. They set a high standard for themselves and those they are leading. This leader wants to do things better and faster, pinpoints poor performers and expects more from them.

| STRENGTHS | WEAKNESSES |
|---|---|
| • Business results quickly achieved<br>• High energy in team<br>• High quality performance<br>• Progressive<br>• Successful | • Can be low on guidance<br>• May lead to exhaustion<br>• Impatience can put team members offside and undercut morale<br>• Team overwhelmed by demands placed on them |

☐ D  ☐ I  ☐ S  ☐ C

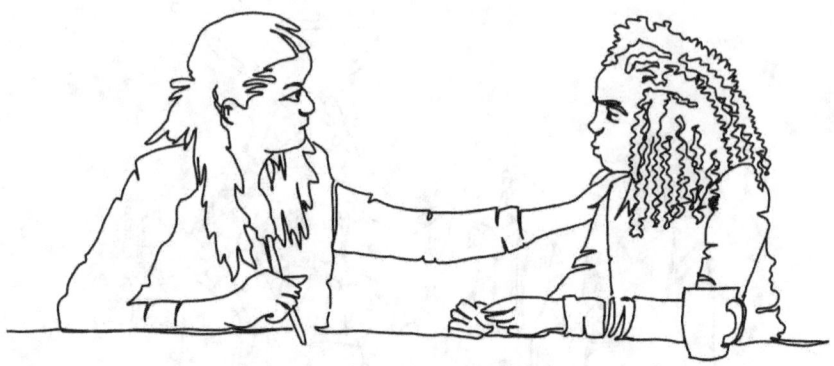

## THE AFFILIATIVE/PATERNALISTIC

Where leaders promote emotional bonds and harmony among teams, help solve conflict and build teams in which members feel connected. This leader creates a family relationship within the group, with the leader the head of the family.

| STRENGTHS | WEAKNESSES |
| --- | --- |
| • Conflicts resolved quickly<br>• Wellbeing of team members becomes a priority<br>• Reduces levels of stress<br>• Team treated as a family environment<br>• Provides good working conditions and employee services<br>• Team works harder out of gratitude | • Conflict and uncomfortable situations avoided<br>• Can reduce team productivity<br>• Can result in complacency<br>• Complex problems may not be faced<br>• Can lose sight of the vision<br>• Requires highly educated and brilliant employees who enjoy this environment |

☐ D   ☐ I   ☐ S   ☐ C

## STYLES NOT TO CHOOSE FROM

### MY WAY OR THE HIGHWAY

This kind of leader wants things to be done in a specific way. From information, processes and decisions, this leader's way is the only way to go and if you do not agree or conform to this leadership style, then you may just find yourself walking all by yourself on the highway!

### THE TICKING TIME BOMB

This leader may always be ready to explode. They are more in their emotional zone and want everything to be done right. They can be somewhat unpredictable at times and may dangerously handle problematic and difficult situations when they arise. When it comes to problems, this leader's actions may be detrimental, resulting in even more problems. BOOM!

### THE HANGER

A kind of leader who is not shy at blaming others and then having them terminated. They leave enough rope for their employees to hang themselves with by not giving proper direction, then blaming them when it's not right. They look like they are hanging loose but in fact they are hanging on by a thread.

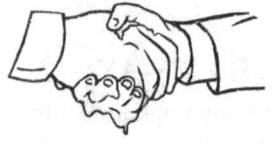

## BAFFLE WITH BULLSHIT RULES

This leader likes to follow rules, and if there isn't a rule for something, they will make one up. You may not know the rule but it will be created for you and you must follow it, even if it seems like bullshit! This leader may make up rules that seem like nonsense and more often than not, they are used to cover unnecessary outcomes or explanations.

From what you have just read, which leadership styles do you like? Which styles can you see yourself implementing to help grow your business, enhance your career, or to lead yourself better and be a leader worth following? Record your thoughts here:

| Style | Strengths |
|---|---|
|  |  |
|  |  |
|  |  |

*"A great leader is waiting inside of each of us, waiting for us to recognize how amazing we can be."*
**Catherine Molloy**

Now that you have identified your strengths and weaknesses, it's time to make a new list. To begin to formulate your own unique style of leadership.

List nine **strengths**, selecting some from your personal list and some from the various Leadership Styles listed.

## MY LEADERSHIP TOOLKIT

Strength #1

Strength #2

Strength #3

Strength #4

Strength #5

Strength #6

Strength #7

Strength #8

..................................................................................................

Strength #9

..................................................................................................

These strengths are indicators of strengths you consciously admire and value, strengths that you want to work on and develop further so you can be the best leader possible.

## EVERYTHING DOMINOS FROM ME

Don't find fault in others. The first rule of conscious leadership is:

> *"Everything dominos from me: find the solution to the problem and lead by example."*
> **Catherine Molloy**

Once you become a more conscious leader, you can tailor a leadership style to suit yourself and your business model. There is a reaction to every action and when we look ahead and around us, we are leading with awareness. By leading ourselves well we can go on to lead others well too.

Mastery of self is the primary goal. This is the first focus.

Bruce Lee became a master of martial arts because of two things, he practiced his craft obsessively and he practiced self-awareness. He also understood that through his relationship with others, he was able to further understand himself.

Lee said, "To know oneself is to study oneself in action with another person. Relationship is a process of self-revelation. Relationship is the mirror in which you discover yourself. To be is to be related."

Therefore relationships, the workplace, friendships and business negotiations are all aspects of learning about yourself and how you relate to the world. Essentially, for every conscious leader, the world in all its chaos and majesty, is the greatest teacher of Self.

Once you realize that everything dominos from the way you relate to the world, to yourself and to others, then the power is yours.

## LEADING IN A TIME OF CRISIS
### *AN INTERVIEW WITH MEREDITH HELLICAR (FORMER CHAIR OF JAMES HARDIE)*

Few business leaders have the breadth of top-level industry experience as Meredith Hellicar. Meredith is ultimately renowned for taking the helm as Chairperson of James Hardie in 2004 and relentlessly steering the company through the blistering asbestos crisis.

I had the pleasure of meeting Meredith when she was a panelist at a conference for the Women Chiefs of Enterprises International in Sydney. She graciously accepted my invitation to be interviewed for this book, and so shared with me the leadership strengths she has admired and cultured in her long career. Qualities that reinforced her deepest convictions during the most testing stretch of her career and ensured the company's "noble goal" was painstakingly achieved by her unfaltering vision.

**Q. Who has been a great leader that you've worked with?**
A great leader I've worked with was George Maltby. George was a long-serving, distinguished public servant, becoming the first Managing Director of the Overseas Telecommunications Commission (OTC) in 1985. He was the most extraordinary human all-in-one…He had a very unusual style in that he made work a combination of a chess game, hand-to-hand combat, a festival and a literary feast.

When George arrived in the mornings, he would walk across the office, passing the staff sitting at their desks and start sprouting a passage from Shakespeare or some other eloquent historical figure that would encapsulate what was going to be the primary focus for the day. He had a quote for everything. By the time he reached his office you knew whether we were going to be creating something that day or fighting a battle for a cause. He was amazing, he brought this energy to every single person he met. Everyone he met was important.

George passed on in 2019 but I believe his secret was that he loved people, the way they worked together, seeing them flourish. He wasn't just about spreading happiness and joy though, he wanted to win by expanding the range of services in the organization, and he was incredibly entrepreneurial. He would think about the manoeuvres that could be made either with his "battalions" or against other people's "battalions."

If there seemed to be barriers to an issue, George would say something like, "Meredith, find a way we can do this! There's got to be a way!" He would think about fifty moves ahead of everyone else.

He just gave of himself to everyone and he'd go along to the Golf Days, the Veterans' Days, the money raising days, supporting everything. Ultimately everything for him was about what humans need; everything was focused around the human emotions, the human interactions. People wanted to work for him because he pulled everyone to him like a magnet. Maybe that was the secret to his leadership. He pulled people to him rather than kept them at a distance and therefore, everybody wanted to help him, to work with him.

Interestingly, by the late '80s, a number of OTC's IT people were being poached by better salary deals elsewhere and George didn't want that to happen. George gave them salary rises, which was in breach of the government wage policy and the Bob Hawke/Paul Keating government sacked George over it! The whole of OTC's workforce went out on strike. Have you ever heard of the rank-and-file of a business striking when the CEO gets sacked?

George never really got over it. He'd given his life to that organization. He didn't want to do anything else. He got appointed to all sorts of telecommunication related things after that but he never returned to another executive role because as he said, "My life was OTC, I couldn't give that same passion anywhere else."

I was very lucky to work with someone like George. He taught me a lot.

**Q. Describe a not so effective leader that you have worked with:**
I can think of someone who I've worked with, and was actually quite fond of, and the media occasionally writes him up as being a fantastic leader because he was just very good at talking the talk.

However he was ineffective because of his inconsistency and spur of the moment decisions. He was opportunistic, with a lack of discipline and frequently distracted by the next shiny object. A leader must be very clear with their team. Your colleagues need to fully understand what your own purpose is, what the business purpose is and where you are heading, so they can head that way too.

Another ineffective trait is a leader who doesn't value working with their team. I don't mean the lone wolf versus team scenario. I'm referring to leaders who run a hub-and-spoke system for the people that report to them. These leaders keep everyone separate from each other, with themselves in the middle and in control of everything. They only tell individuals as much as they need to know to operate, giving them a narrow view of what's involved, rather than recognizing that if you take this diverse group of talented people, you can share all your thoughts and dilemmas knowing you'll end up workshopping a great answer versus that limiting hub-and-spoke system.

A telling difference between effective and ineffective leadership is that a good leader actively seeks out people who are better than they are in each role and is thrilled if they can rise up. A poor leader is going to look for people who aren't a threat; they view the success of others as a threat to their appearance of knowing what they're doing.

There are many factors at play, such as insecurity and a bit of narcissism as they try to cover up their poor leadership traits, in the meantime everyone is telling them how wonderful they are.

A great way to tell if a leader has been really successful is when their people can anticipate what that leader will decide on something and therefore, be able to make that decision for them because the leader has instilled the culture and the values so deeply in the organization, that people know what the right thing to do is. If you don't instil in people what the right thing to do is particular to your business, then it's too late.

**Q. Was there a time you felt you could have led better?**
Yes, I was the Chief Executive of a firm brought in to merge each of the practices around Australia that were working with the same name but were all separate entities. I led myself very well for a period of time in diagnosing what needed to be done for the merger and setting a clear vision, getting everything aligned and through all departments. I think I did well up to a point but then the hard grind of maintaining the message and the momentum struck me.

I found myself getting ground down by some of the behaviors, and I succumbed to it. I forgot all the tenants of leadership that I knew and could offer and understand. I didn't have the willpower, brain space or the confidence (at the time) to know where was the *"me"* that was there in the first year. By the fourth year, I wasn't there.

Values are the glue that sticks a business together. I came to realize I wasn't leading myself well because I didn't align to the values. When you feel your own values are being stripped you need to wonder what are you doing? I felt my values were being undermined by not standing up for them. I discovered you can't work when you're not being true to you. I just felt beaten…it was a heaviness. So after giving a talk on values one day at a business breakfast, I realized that I didn't want to be at the company anymore and went straight up to the Chairman and resigned.

Even though we completed the merger and the business went on to be incredibly successful—my successor that I'd picked and groomed stayed there for 15 odd years—I left with feelings of failure, that I'd led myself badly at the time in that I, well…I wasn't leading at all.

**Q. When have you led yourself well?**
When I took over the chairmanship of James Hardie. I led through all the death threats and everything collapsing around us. I think I really got through this by staying totally true to the purpose and getting the right outcome, knowing it was a sort of noble goal despite what was going on around me.

To find a way of giving people who had contracted asbestosis or mesothelioma sufficient funding for them to survive—this was hardly any compensation for the illness—but given that they deserved the [financial] compensation, we needed to ensure that a fund could be set up that was sustainable but still kept the business alive.

Every manufacturer of asbestos in the United States had gone bankrupt, so the noble goal was to find a way where, forevermore if necessary, there could be an ongoing company *and* an ongoing fund. We just developed a system where 35 percent of free cash flow from the company automatically goes into the fund and it was all achieved amid horrible political circumstances.

It was really, really stressful. Three other directors died during that process, a co-worker committed suicide, a woman had a miscarriage, people were breaking into the office and we had death threats. It was just awful, and so I just had to be absolutely true to what we needed to get done.

**Q. How did you get through this difficult time?**
I kept up with exercise and took regular weekends away. I had a great group of girlfriends who would take me to the north coast to get me away from it all.

Let's review the qualities Meredith Hellicar describes in effective leadership:
- Appreciate and enjoy people working together and seeing them flourish
- Recognize talent and diversity
- Seek out people who are better than they are in their role
- Instil strong culture and values
- Set a clear vision
- Stay true to their purpose

While Meredith Hellicar believes ineffective leaders;
- Are inconsistent
- Lack discipline
- Do not value teams
- Try to control everything
- Lack a clear purpose or direction

- Are often insecure
- Employ people who are not a threat
- View the success of others as threats

Would you agree with this summary? I certainly do. When we start to bring consciousness forward it helps us understand how we need to think and act too. Meredith also highlights the fact that being a conscious leader means we need to be aware of our mental and physical health too.

## LEADERS WE LOOK TO

Think of someone you look towards for leadership in your life. This may be a different person for different aspects of your life. For instance, in my personal life I looked for leadership from my mom, who died when I was 16. When I had children of my own and had to make decisions regarding their wellbeing, I would think, *What would my mom have done?* She was a kind, loving mother and I wanted to emulate her actions.

In my student life, it was my dad who was my mentor. My father had a photographic memory and read thousands of books. If ever I asked him a question, he would usually know the answer but instead of simply telling me, he would draw it out of me. When it came to politics, he had his opinion but he would explain a range of opinions and let us choose. There were four of us in the house and the majority would get the votes! Dad would explain all sides of any discussion, so I had all the facts to help me make my own decisions.

In my business life, I have admired Richard Branson. As he is a high-profile and successful figure across numerous fields of enterprise and business, I discovered that he has various leadership styles which is understandable because a great leader has to draw on many resources; one way does not suit all situations and all people.

However, there is generally one style we favor, especially if we are looking at a situation more from our own perspective and taking into account the other stakeholders. Conscious leadership makes us aware of all sides and everyone involved.

At first, I embraced Branson's leadership style because it felt right to me and we both operated in the people area. His style was generally compatible with my own behavioral style and it was easy for me to implement. His leadership style as a people magnet was natural for me however over time I found some aspects that did not serve me well. I found my leadership was a little chaotic at times and I needed to create systems and processes to achieve control and consistency. Especially when I owned and ran a compliant training company, I needed to develop those skills myself to build a sound business whereas Richard Branson could afford to split up his business into divisions and source the right people for those roles.

When you are conscious of the many aspects of different leadership qualities, you can develop your leadership approach to suit your own behavior style and your situation. I decided to add some traits of a more bureaucratic style of leadership when working in the education system where compliancy is so important. By combining the visionary and charismatic aspects of Richard Branson's leadership style and my own new traits that were now more orderly, I developed a dynamic, conscious style of leadership that worked well for me and helped my business to grow.

Once we understand our own leadership style, we can develop, change and add to it, creating the most appropriate and successful approach for the situation and for the people we are leading.

Whether you are just starting your career or you're well into your journey, whether you are a CEO or founder of your own business, managing teams or a solopreneur, *The Conscious Leader* will give you the skills to truly become a conscious, successful leader in your field, and to help you lead through crises and lead a life worth living.

## CONSCIOUS LEADERS EMERGE THROUGH CRISES

You can often tell who has the ability to lead when shit gets real. When people are panicked or the world is in disarray, leaders emerge. Often in crisis, you can see unique leadership in action.

The 2020 bushfires in Australia saw countless everyday leaders step up and do whatever was required. I can assure you, there was no shortage of so-called "ordinary" people being extraordinary leaders. Time and time again, humble heroes rose from the blackened ashes and forged a new way forward for their community.

With the COVID-19 crisis, businesses and employees all over the world have had their income taken away from them overnight. Countries shut their borders, conferences and group trainings were canceled and business operations were dramatically reduced or forced to close altogether. People were laid off due to revenue loss while those still employed began working from home in lockdown.

Naturally, this left people feeling extremely vulnerable, uncertain of their future and having a harder time seeing the positives.

My business was based on in-person global speaking engagements and workplace training. In many ways most of my business ventures disappeared overnight. I was at the beginning of the fourth year of my five-year plan. Business in 2019 was great and the plan was to continue building on that success. I had spent the past ten years working extremely hard to get where I was.

COVID19 had likely set my business back 5-7 years but I also knew that I didn't want to work seven days a week, nor rebuild a whole new business. So I had to get expansive, conscious and creative, very quickly. There was no time for dwelling IN THE PAST. The playing field had changed overnight and I had to play a new game.

When I think about the differences between the crises that I've experienced, I can see where I led consciously compared to being unconscious in my leadership. For example, with the Global Financial Crisis I swung into action and built my business. I was able to walk out the door in order to meet people and turn those warm leads into hot sales.

I went into autopilot and activated everything I knew, however my focus was on avoiding losing everything I'd built up. I was acting out of fear and not activating myself or being forward-thinking.

This time, through COVID-19, I knew I wouldn't let fear be the driver. I had to be really conscious every time fear wanted to move in and tell me negative lies. Many people have had to think on their feet through this crisis. Some have pivoted their businesses quickly, offering online webinars or programs for free (or very low cost) because their aim is to build their database. Some people were able to access government relief schemes or were thankful to have a partner's income to keep them afloat but even so, for many people, fear was often hovering just out of sight.

As a regular traveler (pre-COVID), I had developed a routine to take care of myself on the road but I underestimated how being grounded due to isolation and throwing myself into very different work, would leave me feeling more tense than usual.

When I first realized that fear was trying to move in, I began asking myself some direct, focused questions:
- How can I use this time and situation purposefully?
- What new skills can I acquire that will help me long-term?
- Where can I be generous with my time?
- How can I help others?

Deliberately focusing on new possibilities gave me purpose to help drive my business and stay motivated. Through taking control of what I could do—getting enough sleep, eating well, self-reflecting on some pointed questions, and leaving my ego behind, I was able to reset my mindset and energy levels.

Now don't get me wrong, this was not an easy shift to make, it was a conscious one. Part of me wanted to yell, "Give me my old life back!" Life with a booming business and flowing economy is much easier than being grounded at home and needing to learn new skills and adapt. I assured my own clients who reached out during this crisis that it's okay to grieve for what has been lost—it's human.

However, the real key is not staying consumed in the grief but pivoting to move forward and creating something new amongst the chaos. It opens up opportunities that many of us may not have had time to explore due to our previous workload. In times of crisis, it's time to *get conscious*. Here's how:

- Reassess your values
- Reassess your direction
- Make plans for the future
- Fill your cup up with things that inspire and motivate you

Now, I'm not suggesting that you fill up your time simply because you have time. It's not about being busy; it's about being conscious of how to use your time wisely. As the philosopher Henry David Thoreau so aptly said, "It is not enough to be busy; so are the ants. The question is: What are we busy about?"

So I encourage you to make goals and plans that lift you up and move you forward.

Learn new skills and adapt to the changing times as much as you can. You're not alone. As I write this book, I am going through the exact same process. If I ever feel discouraged, I think of a quote from the integral character, Andy in *The Shawshank Redemption,* "I guess it comes down to a simple choice really. Get busy living or get busy dying."

A conscious leader gets busy living.

## CONSCIOUSNESS CREATES CHANGE

Be the leader you want to see in the world.

Think of all the people you consider great leaders. You may think of the likes of Martin Luther King Junior, Mahatma Gandhi, Nelson Mandela and Mother Teresa. Others think of new and emerging leaders like the young Pakistani education activist Malala Yousafzai or Swedish environmental activist Greta Thunberg. Others prefer business leaders such as Steve Jobs or Bill Gates. When I think of great leaders,

I think of my compassionate and nurturing parents and the dynamic Richard Branson.

Whoever you identify with, now consider what makes them so great? It's not a question of whether they are all truly great leaders or not, the question is what makes them great to *you*? What traits do you admire and respect? What symbolizes leadership to you? Is it their values, or actions, or humility? Their courage, altruism or perseverance? I think all of these great leaders each offer a strength we can aspire to emulate in our own lives and leadership arenas.

To use the famous Gandhi quote, "Be the change you want to see in the world."

Former Unilever CEO Paul Polman is known around the world as a conscious business leader. What makes him so well-known is his willingness to call things out and open up much needed conversations. He leads by example and promotes conscious business leadership.

For example, when he was hired as the CEO of Unilever, he rolled out the Unilever Sustainable Living Plan to implement a more socially responsible approach to business. This was a detailed plan in how the company would reduce carbon emissions, source more sustainable products and alter the impact to the environment. He spoke passionately about climate change, lifting the standard of living for the impoverished and pledged to halve the environmental impact of Unilever's products by 2020.

Polman decided that Unilever would not publish profit updates every quarter, as this encouraged short-term thinking, which was not part of their new culture and creed. He even encouraged short-term style shareholders to not invest in them if they didn't value Unilever's long-term business model. In short, he created a new type of business model. He saw the need for change and had the guts to go out and do the tough work.

Of course not everybody has to be like Paul Polman. Not everybody has the ingenuity, education or experience to take on the world heavyweights in business and give them a masterclass in Corporate Social Responsibility. However in many interviews, Paul Polman announces that leaders are everywhere in the community and they aren't always the ones in obvious leadership roles. They are the ones driven by purpose and have the determination to make necessary changes.

Mother Teresa didn't get up and say, "Hey, I'm a leader, everyone follow me." Instead, she pursued what she felt was necessary to make change and went humbly about her business. People were inspired by her actions and wanted to join in her cause. Gandhi's stance on non-violence and Martin Luther King's stance on equality sparked the same influence. People want to join important causes and escalate the message to new heights. Therefore, leadership is not a person per se but qualities you can cultivate through the choices you make every day.

How you lead has an impact on how people respond to you and how successful you are in your role. The starting point is to understand how you lead best and to assess what characteristics may be holding you back from being the best version of yourself as a leader. This will then help determine which skills you would like to add to your toolkit for becoming an outstanding leader.

## LOOK TO THE LEADERS YOU ADMIRE

Think about leaders you admire—they might be in business, politics or could be teachers or emergency workers. Once you have chosen your leader, look closely at their leadership style and ask yourself why you chose that leader, and what aspect of their leadership style would suit you.

You might choose a leader but not like all the aspects of their leadership style. For instance, in the section on "Leading Yourself" I pointed out that in my business life I have always looked towards Richard Branson's style of leadership but found aspects of it that didn't suit my business model. I substituted these aspects with a more bureaucratic style of compliancy to meet the government criteria in the education field.

Learning to lead well is a continual learning process. You need to choose your tools and style to match the people and projects you are leading.

There is never a one style approach to every situation, but more there is a situational approach to leadership and it involves knowing yourself and understanding others.

In other words, there is a domino effect that comes through leading yourself well and having the ability to lead others well too, so it is important to be conscious of the outcomes you desire from the beginning.

Don't look for fault in others; let's get our own house in order first. Remember:

**Everything dominos from me:**
**find the solution to the problem and lead by example.**

CHAPTER 2

# BEING CONSCIOUS OF EMOTIONAL INTELLIGENCE

## WHY IS THIS SO IMPORTANT? BECOMING A NEW CEIL

*"Personal power comes from using the right emotion at the right time."*
**Catherine Molloy**

Once you understand your leadership style you immediately become more self-aware of the way you think, behave and treat others. You understand your strengths and weaknesses, your inclinations and blind spots with a deeper awareness. This puts you ahead of the game in both leadership and emotional intelligence.

Much has been said and written about Emotional Intelligence (often referred to as EI or EQ)

Emotional Intelligence first appeared in a 1964 paper *The Communication of Emotional Meaning* by Joel Robert Davitz and Michael Beldoch,[1] and was further defined by Peter Salovey and John Mayer in 1989, as "the ability to monitor one's own and other people's emotions, to discriminate between different emotions and label them appropriately, and to use emotional information to guide thinking and behavior."[2] This definition was further refined into four abilities:

- Perceiving
- Using
- Understanding
- Managing emotions

These abilities are considered by Salovely and Mayer as "distinct yet related."[3]

Emotional Intelligence then gained mainstream popularity with the 1995 best-selling book *Emotional Intelligence: Why It Can Matter More Than IQ*[4] and EQ was catapulted into the mainstream business sector in new and exciting ways. Leaders and management personnel started to look at the need to use and enhance EQ and understand that it wasn't just about emotions, it helped understand staff, manage conflict and bring out the best in oneself. It became a business methodology and built stronger bonds and brands.

My passion with EQ started when I was traveling at age nineteen, exploring new cultures and meeting people from all walks of life, but it was through my career that I was able to explore it deeper. I was working at the Commercial Bank of Australia after they had just merged with The Bank of NSW, and they released VHS training videos on understanding body language and team building (yes, VHS players were "modern" back then). I took the videos home and consumed them, I loved knowing more about how we communicate without even saying a word. Putting what I had learned into practice, I quickly ended up as the top selling salesperson for Queensland, followed shortly with smashing sales Australia-wide. I had been intuitively working my soft skills in EQ for years, but had never understood what it was academically labelled until the book *Emotional Intelligence* was released. It was a lightbulb moment—*ahhh, there is a label for this.*

The research made sense to me and gave me a framework to work with and ultimately teach others. It gave me context to my inner experiences and helped me feel understood and validated in the corporate world.

## WHAT IS EMOTIONAL INTELLIGENCE?

Emotional Intelligence is the ability to be aware of our emotions, understand and manage our emotions and be aware of and understand the emotions of and manage the emotions of others.

*What are emotions?*

Emotions are strong feelings about how we feel or experience our world. Feelings can change from moment to moment depending on our surroundings, what is happening in our daily lives with our families, friends, work mates, and sport mates, etc. How we interact with others is affected by how we feel and how the person(s) we are interacting with feel. How other people interact with us depends on how they feel and on how we react to their interaction with us. So, if feelings affect our interaction with others, strong feelings or emotions can accentuate these interactions in our day-to-day relationships. By focusing on positive emotions such as excitement, happiness, pride, and eliminating negative emotions such as anger, fear and stress, we can work towards developing better Emotional Intelligence.

> "Organisations that value and widely use Emotional Intelligence are 3.2x more effective at leadership development."[5]

# EMOTIONAL INTELLIGENCE MODELS

To understand how to become emotionally intelligent, I will introduce you to various Emotionally Intelligent Models. There are several pioneering models to explore.

1. Ability Model
2. Mixed Model and Daniel Goleman's Adjusted Model
3. Trait Model
4. Bar-On-Model
5. Genos Model

| Name of Model | What is says | Who developed it |
|---|---|---|
| The Ability Model | Defines emotional intelligence as 'the ability to perceive emotions, integrate emotions to facilitate thoughts, understand emotions and regulate emotions to promote personal growth.' | Peter Salovey and John Mayer |
| The Mixed Model | Identifies five (5) key competencies that make up emotional intelligence.<br>1. Self-awareness<br>2. Self-regulation<br>3. Motivation<br>4. Empathy<br>5. Social skills | Daniel Goleman 1995 |
| | Goleman adjusted his model to include only four (4) dimensions instead of the original five (5)<br>1. Self-awareness<br>2. Self-management<br>3. Social awareness<br>4. Relationship management | Daniel Goleman 2002 |

| The Trait Model | Evaluates how an individual perceives their emotional skills and abilities. | Konstantinos Vasilis Petrides |
|---|---|---|
| The Bar-On-Model | Describes emotional intelligence as 'an array of interrelated emotional and social competencies, skills and behaviors that impact intelligent behavior.' | Reuven Bar-On |
| The Genos Model | Lists seven (7) core skills including:<br>1. Self-awareness<br>2. Awareness of others<br>3. Expression<br>4. Reasoning<br>5. Self-management<br>6. Management of others<br>7. Self-control | Dr Ben Palmer and Professor Con Stough |

The models and ideas are extremely well researched and tested. I have looked at them all in great detail but instead of you having to delve deep into each model, I can save you some time and let you know that generally, in most of the models are similar categories and outcomes. They basically boil down to four key areas:

- **Self-awareness:** being aware of your own emotions
- **Self-management:** being able to manage your own emotions
- **Social awareness:** being aware of emotions of others
- **Relationship management:** the management of others, maintaining relationships, leadership

More currently in 2016, researchers from John Carroll University, Texas University and Cleveland Leadership Center, Scott J. Allen, Marcy Levy Shankman and Paige Haber-Curran conducted some excellent research relating to the necessary components to fully optimize Emotional Intelligence Leadership. This type of research is right up my alley and as it includes Consciousness, Emotional Intelligence and Leadership.

The researchers broke down nineteen core EQ capacities into three main groups. Here's a snapshot of their findings.
- **Consciousness of Self:** self-perception, self-control, optimism, achievement, self-esteem, flexibility, among others.
- **Consciousness of Others:** empathy, inspiring and enhancing others, building teams, facilitating change, coaching, among others.
- **Consciousness of Context:** analyzing group dynamics and assessing the environment.[6]

Developing these capacities position you as an emotionally intelligent leader and give you a lifelong journey in self-improvement. You can download the full list of these 19 Capacities in my Interactive book.

|  | Observing | Doing |
|---|---|---|
| **Consciousness of Self** <br> Personal competence | Self-awareness | Self-management |
| **Consciousness of Others** <br> Social competence | Social awareness | Relationship management |
| **Consciousness of Context** <br> Environmental competence | Environmental awareness | Managing wider dynamics and trends |

The researchers who developed this—Scott J. Allen, Marcy Levy Shankman, Paige Haber-Curran use the metaphor of the Wi-Fi signal strength. The signal strength represents one's ability to connect. They suggest to place yourself at the center of the dot and see each bar as the areas: Consciousness of Self, Consciousness of Others and Consciousness of Context.

They say, "One bar of signal strength will work, but there is often static and noise, and things may move slowly. Additional bars indicate a better connection and result in better performance. We suggest that generally speaking, working with all three bars at full strength will allow an individual to more effectively connect with and engage others."[7]

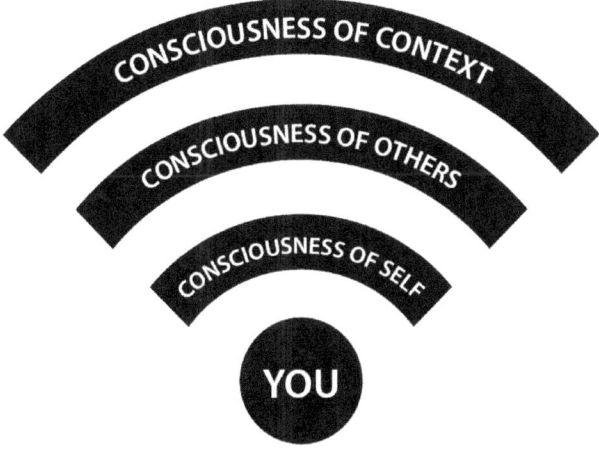

You will see that by working consciously within these frameworks and mindset, a new type of leader will emerge. (More on that soon. Stay tuned).

# CONSCIOUSNESS OF SELF
## SELF-AWARENESS

Being conscious of how to behave and operate is critical to becoming a Conscious Leader.

Self-awareness has been described as the ability to:
- recognize your own emotions and how they affect your thoughts and behavior.
- know your strengths and weaknesses and have self-confidence.

But why is this important? The idea is that you need to recognize your own emotions, understand how these emotions affect your thoughts and behaviors, so you are able to manage them. Sounds easy on paper, right? But it can be a whole other ball game in real-life. Why? Because we all have emotional triggers. We all have little irks and issues that push our buttons. We have personal likes and dislikes and life doesn't balk around you or your preferences.

## EMOTIONAL TRIGGERS PULL THE REACTION GUN

Emotional triggers are situations that trigger emotions and therefore reactions. You need to be aware of your emotional triggers to help control your emotional response or reactions to situations.

Triggers can set off our emotions like a firecracker if we're not aware, it could be as simple as a poorly-phrased word from someone, or their volume or tone of voice that results in you going from being as cool as a cucumber to fiery-hot like a chili-pepper. Emotional triggers move our emotions up and down the spectrum.

Identifying your triggers and recognizing when they show up in your body is a good practice to becoming conscious and self-aware. The more tuned into yourself you are, the more conscious you become, and with further practice, this becomes an innate habit.

Learning to feel the "heat rise" in you as someone angers you could be the first sign of what is occurring. It's all about being aware of what is occurring rather than reacting blindly as it takes you by surprise.

Examples of triggers that can occur at home or work can include:
- A look such as uplifted eyebrows (here we go again), rolling eyes (really!), wandering eyes (distracted).
- Poor listening skills can show up when the answer to the question asked by the listener was given moments ago by the speaker (this excludes digging down for more information).
- One person may be more emotionally intelligent than the other person (less likely to react immediately).
- Tone, pitch or volume of voice. (Think a warm, genuine "thank you" versus one with a flat unemotional tone).
- Avoiding eye contact or being distracted (checking your phone or texting while someone is talking).
- Nodding before the speaker has finished what they are saying.
- Nodding and saying yes without looking at the speaker.
- Talking without checking whether they have the listener's attention first.

All of the above can leave one party of the conversation feeling unheard or misunderstood.

Now, of course, in the workplace for example, if someone is sitting at their desk it doesn't mean that they are open for business for whoever arrives. They may be deep in a task and need time to switch their attention and mindset from what they were doing to what's being presented.

Make sure you have the other person's undivided attention. Ask if they have a moment, or can you make a time with them later to talk. Be aware when you ask to speak with someone of their emotional needs— are they the type of person who will need to discuss it immediately, or are they more comfortable to take time out to discuss it later in the day.

Being mindful (not mind-full) is always a positive behavior.

As Mahatma Gandhi said:

> "Carefully watch your thoughts, for they become
> your words. Manage and watch your words,
> for they will become your actions.
> Consider and judge your actions,
> for they have become your habits.
> Acknowledge and watch your habits,
> for they shall become your values.
> Understand and embrace your values,
> for they become your destiny."

We will learn more about how to control your emotional triggers in Chapter 6.

**Bonus Video**
See Catherine's video on how to change your state immediately in the interactive version of *The Conscious Leader*.

# SELF-MANAGEMENT

How we manage ourselves is paramount to increasing our emotional intelligence and leadership qualities. Self-management is described as:

'The ability to:
- control impulsive feelings and behaviors
- manage your emotions in a healthy way
- follow through on commitments
- adapt to changing situations.'[8]

We saw that by being aware of your emotional triggers both in your personal life and workplace life is the first key to self-awareness. Next comes self-management. In effect, if you take time to observe and control your impulsive feelings and behaviors, then you can begin to manage your emotions in a healthy and positive way.

Two effective ways to self-manage our emotions are through:
1. self-reflection
2. feedback

## SELF-REFLECTION

Self-reflection is the process of reviewing and reflecting on your behavior and actions. Using self-reflection you can:
- Identify the triggers that lead you to your emotions
- Align your thoughts and ideas to be more positive
- Reflect how your emotions affect your job performance
- Aim to understand your strengths, weaknesses and limitations
- Aim to gain confidence about things you do well
- Recognize which of your emotions you feel you need to focus on to improve and be positive
- Identify which emotions you may need help with to help you improve
- Focus on changing your future behaviors through focusing on positive emotions

A good time to self-reflect is at the end of each day. Sit quietly and reflect on the events of the day.
- Think of three positive and three negative interactions you encountered during the day.
- Reflect on the emotions you felt for each interaction.
- Reflect on the positive emotions and why they happened, then consider the negative emotions and how these could have been turned into positive emotions.

You can journal your feelings and new-found awareness or even keep a lovely notebook of thoughts and reflections for you to look back on.

**3 Positive Interactions**

Emotion 1: ......................................................................................

Emotion 2: ......................................................................................

Emotion 3: ......................................................................................

**3 Negative Interactions**

Emotion 1: ......................................................................................

Emotion 2: ......................................................................................

Emotion 3: ......................................................................................

How could these negatives be turned into positives:

..........................................................................................................

..........................................................................................................

..........................................................................................................

..........................................................................................................

..........................................................................................................

# FEEDBACK

Feedback is critical in developing your self-awareness and management. Feedback gives you information about what you do well and where you could improve. It allows you to:
- reflect on your performance from the perspective of others
- understand any emotional strengths and weaknesses you have
- clarify any inconsistencies in your actions and emotions
- consider any changes you think you may need to make to achieve better outcomes

Feedback can be formal or informal. Formal feedback normally happens in arranged meetings used for the sole purpose of giving feedback. In a work situation these can be work group meetings, individual performance appraisal meetings or a meeting arranged for the specific purpose of giving formal feedback. Informal feedback usually happens on a day-to-day basis.

**There are four main types of feedback:** positive feedback, constructive feedback, negative feedback and destructive feedback.

**Positive feedback** aims to reinforce good behavior or outcomes. To get positive feedback you would receive information on how and why your actions resulted in a positive outcome.

*"You have done excellent this year Muhammad. Your ability to keep customers happy and drive sales every month has resulted in both a financially prosperous year and a happier workplace for all."*

**Constructive feedback** builds upon experience. It provides steps for any future experiences. Constructive feedback is important as it often gives a person a sense of achievement and motivates them to improve further.

Constructive feedback involves: giving positive feedback on performance outcomes achieved. Stating clearly the performance outcomes that were not achieved. Ask questions as to why these performance outcomes have not been achieved and possible solutions for them to be achieved.

Discuss future approaches to performance standards and finish on a positive note.

*"It's great to take this time to catch up and see how you are going. I feel like you haven't been as happy at work lately. I'd like to know how you are feeling and if there something I can do to help you have a better experience here?"*

**Negative feedback** usually happens in the workplace when a person has not achieved their required outcomes. It is extremely important how negative feedback is delivered. A good technique is to state the negative feedback but follow up with positive or constructive feedback.

For example, *"Jeremy, you failed to achieve your targets this week. Perhaps if you tried to concentrate on doing the activities you are good at, maybe next week you will do better."*

**Destructive feedback** is where one person puts the blame on another person for not achieving. Destructive feedback is often harsh and very demotivating.

For example, *"You made the lowest targets this week, less than any other week. If you continue like this you will not have a job."*

By continuously employing self-management techniques and constantly reflecting on situations and gaining feedback, you will gain the tools to adapt to changing situations. Keeping good notes and diaries and maintaining regular check-ins and performance-based meetings is a great start. Role-playing how to give and receive feedback is also an effective workplace practice.

## CONSCIOUSNESS OF OTHERS
## SOCIAL AWARENESS

Social awareness is about understanding the needs and concerns of other people, and handling them appropriately. This includes such traits as empathy and understanding, consideration for how others fit in within the workplace and meeting the needs of customers and clients.

Social awareness has been described by Goleman as the ability to:
- observe and understand the emotions, needs and concerns of other people
- pick up on emotional cues
- feel comfortable socially and recognize the power dynamics in a group or organisation.

Most workplaces today are diverse, made up of individuals from different cultural, social and educational backgrounds. As a worker you need to learn how to respect these differences. To understand diversity in the workplace you need to look at the following:

- **Diversity** is the individual differences in people. Workplace diversity includes race, ethnicity, gender, age, religion, sexual orientation and ability. Being intelligent about diversity is now one the most important attributes in the workplace.
- **Inclusion** is the level of involvement of people within a workplace. Those with diverse backgrounds should have the same opportunities as all other workers. An emotionally intelligent leader will make sure that everyone is involved equally in daily workplace activities.
- **Cultural Competence** is the ability of a workplace to respond to the needs of a culturally diverse workforce and customer base. This may mean writing, developing and implementing policies and providing training to increase the ability of the workplace to take account of language differences and the cultural needs of all workers.
- **Cultural Intelligence** is the ability of a leader to operate within and help a diverse work team to work together. A culturally intelligent leader should understand and respect cultural differences and empathize and be flexible when interacting with all workers.

A diverse workplace results in many benefits to a workplace and is usually more efficient, productive and profitable.

In Australia by law, workplaces must comply with Equal Employment Opportunities legislation to provide a discrimination and harassment free workplace. Diversity and inclusion means employing a broad range of people. Each worker is valued and respected equally regardless of their race, ethnicity, gender, sexual orientation, religion or ability.

| Aspect | Explanation |
|---|---|
| Age | You should recruit people of all ages, from school leavers to mature aged (16–70). |
| Culture | People come from different countries and have different cultural beliefs, practices and work ethics. |
| Race | Race refers to the ancestry or genetic background of a person. It is important to note that this can be different from a person's culture, for example a person with parents from China could be born and raised in Australia and so identifies as an Australian. |
| Ethnicity | A workplace will be comprised of people from different countries who speak a variety of languages and have different ways of eating, communicating and dressing. |
| Gender | The balance of male to female employees will depend on the nature of your workplace and work, however it is important not to stereotype ability due to gender, for example there are many competent female builders and male nurses. |
| Religion | Individuals have different religious beliefs and some may have none at all. Religions have their own holidays for worship as well as times of day for prayer and this should be provided for as appropriate. |
| Sexuality | Individuals will have different sexual orientations, including heterosexual, homosexual or bisexual. |
| Education & Ability | Within your work group there could be people with basic education as well as those highly qualified. Some people might have learning disabilities that affect their ability to conduct certain tasks. Everyone will have different levels of ambition and aptitude. |

| | |
|---|---|
| Personality | We all have different personalities such as introverted or extroverted, creative or logical. Our personalities often determine our preferences, strengths and weaknesses in the workplace. |
| Language | English is not the first language for many people. You might also have members in your team who use other forms of communication, such as sign language. |
| Family structure | Your family situation can influence how you approach your life, including your career. Family arrangements can include married, single, de-facto or separated. A work group member might be a single parent or have no children. |

This understanding of social awareness helps broaden perceptions and provides emotionally safe workplaces for everyone.

# RELATIONSHIP MANAGEMENT

Relationships are the most powerful things in our world. When they work well, they are incredible. When they don't, they can be challenging and toxic. It's important to develop your capacity to manage relationships positively in your work and home life.

Relationship management is the ability to:
- Develop and maintain good relationships
- Communicate clearly
- Inspire and influence others
- Work well in a team
- Manage conflict

> *"Great relationships are about two things:
> First, appreciating the similarities,
> and second, respecting the differences."*
> **Anonymous**

A good example of relationship management stems back to the 1800s by John Wanamaker renowned as the king of retail service. He is credited for inventing the humble price-tag and making it an industry standard.

One day while walking through his store in Philadelphia, he noticed a customer waiting to be served. No one from the store was serving her or even looking in her direction. His salespeople were all having fun talking amongst themselves. He quietly went behind the sales counter and served the waiting customer himself. Then smiled and he handed the customer's purchase to his salespeople asking it to be wrapped. Then, he went on his way.

Wanamaker was later quoted as saying: "I learned thirty years ago that it is foolish to scold people. I have enough trouble overcoming my own limitations without fretting over the fact that God has not seen fit to distribute evenly the gift of intelligence."

Moral: Don't criticize others when they don't meet your standards; instead lead by example. Relationship management is all about building good rapport whilst not forgetting you as the leader can show how it's done.

Let's not forget that Emotional Intelligence can be taught and modeled. The most effective leaders have been found to have a high degree of emotional intelligence. For example, Motorola manufacturing plant utilized stress-reduction and emotional-intelligence programs and as a result, 93% of their employees became more productive.

## CONSCIOUSNESS OF CONTEXT

Being conscious of context is often a forgotten factor but it's important to see things from a wider perspective and understand how everything works and fits together. It gives context to the smaller moving parts within the broader framework.

This involves things such as:
- Analyzing the group
- Interpreting group dynamics
- Assessing the environment
- Interpreting external forces and trends

Seeing ourselves and others in the broader framework of our environment gives us vision and extends the lense of our observation. For example, understanding how your team works together is important, but seeing, analysing and interpreting their deeper group dynamics within the team is more nuanced.

Understanding external forces and trends within your environment is to be conscious of the larger context in which your business operates and the influences imposed on it, both positive and negative.

**What Is Your Level of Emotional Intelligence?**

If you'd like to know your current level of Emotional Intelligence, then I have hand crafted a fun quiz for you to explore. Simply complete the quiz below or online in the Bonus Interactive Book at deanpublishing.com/consciousleader.

# QUIZ: ARE YOU A CONSCIOUS EMOTIONALLY INTELLIGENT LEADER?

**Question 1:** For each of the following workplace situations, tick the ones you think create stress.

| Workplace state | Creates stress | Does not create stress |
|---|---|---|
| Too many jobs expected to be completed | | |
| Adequate time allowed to complete a job | | |
| Having no job description | | |
| Providing training to complete a job | | |

**Question 2:** Which of the following actions do you use when making decisions. Tick the relevant box.

| Action | Use | Do not use |
|---|---|---|
| Active listening | | |
| Reflection before speaking | | |
| Observing non-verbal cues of team members | | |
| Observing emotional cues of team members | | |
| Observing interactions between members | | |

**Question 3:** Match the following signs of stress with the type of stress, for example, crying = emotional stress. *Signs of stress: Losing weight, smoking or smoking more than usual, forgetfulness, lack of motivation.*

| Type of stress | Sign of stress |
|---|---|
| Physical | |
| Emotional | |
| Mental | |
| Behavioral | |

**Question 4:** Using a score of 0 to 2 (0 = Poor, 1 = Good and 2 = Excellent), score how well you believe your team performs by ticking the relevant box.

| Performance | 0 | 1 | 2 |
|---|---|---|---|
| Loyalty to team | | | |
| Trusting each other | | | |
| Respectful of each other i.e. showing empathy and active listening | | | |
| Problem solving collaboratively | | | |
| Adapting easily to change | | | |
| Effectively handling pressure | | | |

**Question 5:** Where constructive behaviors trigger positive emotions and destructive behaviors trigger negative emotions, decide which of the following behaviors are constructive and destructive by ticking the relevant box.

| Behavior | Constructive | Destructive |
|---|---|---|
| Aggression | | |
| Discussion | | |
| Honesty | | |
| Inclusion | | |
| Judging | | |
| Listening actively | | |
| Questioning lots | | |
| Sarcasm | | |
| Being proactive | | |
| Being focused | | |

**Question 6:** Match the following comments with the types of feedback. *Types of feedback: Positive, Constructive, Negative, Destructive*

| Comment | Types of feedback |
|---|---|
| Well you nearly got it, try this | |
| That's the wrong way to do it, try this | |
| Excellent, what a great job | |
| That is awful, just fix it or else | |

**Question 7:** As a leader tick any of the following actions you take.

| Action | Yes I do this | I do this sometimes | No I do not do this |
|---|---|---|---|
| Being a role model | | | |
| Provide training in handling emotions | | | |
| Actively promoting inclusion | | | |
| Encourage workers to exercise | | | |
| Praise a job well done | | | |

**Question 8:** Do you use any of the following activities as a team leader? Tick the appropriate box.

| Activity | Yes I use | No I do not use |
|---|---|---|
| Team meetings | | |
| Team member reviews | | |
| One-on-one reviews | | |
| Training in self-reflection | | |
| Team feedback reviews | | |

**Question 9:** Which of the following best describes the decision-making processes you follow? Tick the relevant box.

| | |
|---|---|
| Including team members in decision-making | |
| Allowing teams to make decisions | |
| Making decisions based on evaluating options | |

**Question 10:** For each of the following emotions tick if you think it is a strength or a weakness.

| Emotion | Strength | Weakness |
|---|---|---|
| Anger | | |
| Anxiety | | |
| Diplomacy | | |
| Empathy | | |
| Enthusiasm | | |
| Fear | | |
| Frustration | | |
| Open-mindedness | | |
| Optimism | | |
| Compassion | | |
| Discretion | | |
| Broad-mindedness | | |

**Question 11:** Do you actively employ any of the following as a team leader? Tick the most relevant.

| Action | I do this | I do this sometimes | I do not do this |
|---|---|---|---|
| Encourage team members to work on a work /life balance | | | |
| Support team members to identify their emotional state | | | |
| Provide training on identifying emotional triggers | | | |
| Maintaining emotional composure | | | |
| Communicate openly with team members | | | |
| Select projects to maximize team strengths | | | |
| Allocate tasks based on emotional strengths | | | |
| Encourage team members to report mistakes | | | |
| Give on-going constructive feedback | | | |
| Reward outstanding achievements in teams | | | |
| Reward outstanding achievements of individuals | | | |

| | | | |
|---|---|---|---|
| Celebrate successful team outcomes | | | |

**Question 12:** Tick any of the following actions you take when dealing with conflict in the workplace.

| Action | Yes I do this | I do this sometimes | No I do not do this |
|---|---|---|---|
| Listen to both sides of the conflict | | | |
| If anger arises allow both parties to vent it | | | |
| Prioritize issues causing emotional stress | | | |
| Decide on the outcome | | | |

## HOW TO TALLY UP YOUR SCORE

Go through the 12 questions and tally up your points under each question based on where you have placed your ticks.

# SCORING

## Question 1

| Workplace state | Creates stress | Does not create stress |
|---|---|---|
| Too many jobs expected to be completed | 1 | 0 |
| Adequate time allowed to complete a job | 0 | 1 |
| Having no job description | 1 | 0 |
| Providing training to complete a job | 0 | 1 |

My Score: /4

## Question 2

| Action | Use | Do not use |
|---|---|---|
| Active listening | 1 | 0 |
| Reflection before speaking | 1 | 0 |
| Observing non-verbal cues of team members | 1 | 0 |
| Observing emotional cues of team members | 1 | 0 |
| Observing interactions between members | 1 | 0 |

My Score: /5

### Question 3

| Type of stress | Sign of stress | Score |
|---|---|---|
| Physical | Losing weight | 1 |
| Emotional | Lack of motivation | 1 |
| Mental | Forgetfulness | 1 |
| Behavioral | Smoking or smoking more | 1 |

My Score: /4

### Question 4

| Performance | Score | | |
|---|---|---|---|
| Loyalty to team | 0 | 1 | 2 |
| Trusting each other | 0 | 1 | 2 |
| Respectful of each other i.e. showing empathy and active listening | 0 | 1 | 2 |
| Problem solving collaboratively | 0 | 1 | 2 |
| Adapting easily to change | 0 | 1 | 2 |
| Effectively handling pressure | 0 | 1 | 2 |

My Score: /12

## Question 5

| Behavior | Constructive | Destructive |
|---|---|---|
| Aggression | 0 | 1 |
| Discussion | 1 | 0 |
| Honesty | 1 | 0 |
| Inclusion | 1 | 0 |
| Judging | 0 | 1 |
| Listening actively | 1 | 0 |
| Questioning lots | 0 | 1 |
| Sarcasm | 0 | 1 |
| Being proactive | 1 | 0 |
| Being focused | 1 | 0 |

My Score: /10

## Question 6

| Comment | Types of feedback | Score |
|---|---|---|
| Well you nearly got it, try this | Constructive | 1 |
| That's the wrong way to do it, try this | Negative | 1 |
| Excellent, what a great job | Positive | 1 |
| That is awful, just fix it or else | Destructive | 1 |

My Score: /4

## Question 7

| Action | Yes I do this | I do this sometimes | No I do not do this |
|---|---|---|---|
| Being a role model | 2 | 1 | 0 |
| Provide training in handling emotions | 2 | 1 | 0 |
| Actively promoting inclusion | 2 | 1 | 0 |
| Encourage workers to exercise | 2 | 1 | 0 |
| Praise a job well done | 2 | 1 | 0 |

My Score: /10

## Question 8

| Activity | Yes I use | No I do not use |
|---|---|---|
| Team meetings | 1 | 0 |
| Team member reviews | 1 | 0 |
| One-on-one reviews | 1 | 0 |
| Training in self-reflection | 1 | 0 |
| Team feedback reviews | 1 | 0 |

My Score: /5

## Question 9

|  | Score |
|---|---|
| Including team members in decision-making | 2 |
| Allowing teams to make decisions | 1 |
| Making decisions based on evaluating options | 0 |

My Score: /2

## Question 10

| Emotion | Strength | Weakness |
|---|---|---|
| Anger | 0 | 1 |
| Anxiety | 0 | 1 |
| Diplomacy | 1 | 0 |
| Empathy | 1 | 0 |
| Enthusiasm | 1 | 0 |
| Fear | 0 | 1 |
| Frustration | 0 | 1 |
| Open-mindedness | 1 | 0 |
| Optimism | 1 | 0 |
| Compassion | 1 | 0 |
| Discretion | 1 | 0 |
| Broad-mindedness | 1 | 0 |

My Score: /12

## Question 11

| Action | I do this | I do this sometimes | I do not do this |
|---|---|---|---|
| Encourage team members to work on a work /life balance | 2 | 1 | 0 |
| Support team members to identify their emotional state | 2 | 1 | 0 |
| Provide training on identifying emotional triggers | 2 | 1 | 0 |
| Maintaining emotional composure | 2 | 1 | 0 |
| Communicate openly with team members | 2 | 1 | 0 |
| Select projects to maximize team strengths | 2 | 1 | 0 |
| Allocate tasks based on emotional strengths | 2 | 1 | 0 |
| Encourage team members to report mistakes | 2 | 1 | 0 |
| Give on-going constructive feedback | 2 | 1 | 0 |
| Reward outstanding achievements in teams | 2 | 1 | 0 |
| Reward outstanding achievements of individuals | 2 | 1 | 0 |

| Action | Yes I do this | I do this sometimes | No I do not do this |
|---|---|---|---|
| Celebrate successful team outcomes | 2 | 1 | 0 |

My Score: /24

## Question 12

| Action | Yes I do this | I do this sometimes | No I do not do this |
|---|---|---|---|
| Listen to both sides of the conflict | 2 | 1 | 0 |
| If anger arises allow both parties to vent it | 2 | 1 | 0 |
| Prioritize issues causing emotional stress | 2 | 1 | 0 |
| Decide on the outcome | 2 | 1 | 0 |

My Score: /8

## TOTALS

| Question | Maximum score | My score |
|---|---|---|
| 1 | 4 | |
| 2 | 5 | |
| 3 | 4 | |
| 4 | 12 | |
| 5 | 10 | |
| 6 | 4 | |
| 7 | 10 | |
| 8 | 5 | |
| 9 | 2 | |
| 10 | 12 | |
| 11 | 24 | |
| 12 | 8 | |
| **TOTAL** | 100 | |

## OUTCOME

**0–30 points**
You have low emotional intelligence

**30–60 points**
You have moderate evidence of emotional intelligence

**60–80 points**
You have a high level of emotional intelligence

**80–100 points**
You have exceptionally high levels of emotional intelligence

## THE PROBLEM WITH KNOWING VERSUS DOING

*What were your results?*

I can tell you that the average person marks high in emotional intelligence because we understand the way we're meant to act, however, what we know and what we do are two different things.

Did you take the quiz based on what you KNOW? Go and take the test again, but this time complete the quiz based on your actions, how you react, what you actually do on daily basis.

*Did your results change the second time? What was the main difference between them?*

When I first set up my own training company in 2009 and became accredited to teach the Diploma of Leadership Management I discovered that people were able to pass the Emotional Intelligence unit quite easily, but when it came to applying it in the workplace and something didn't go their way, they defaulted to reacting with emotion. Some pouted and complained, others became withdrawn and isolated, some blamed other people more than themselves. Without being conscious, they were unable to handle conflict or lead successfully. As I said, it's one thing to know emotional intelligence, but another to put it into daily practice and *be* it.

An important part of emotional intelligence is the ability to be self-aware and reflect on your actions and behaviors.

---

Did you know that Emotional Intelligence accounts for nearly 90 percent of what moves people up the career ladder when their IQ and technical skills are similar![9]

## CEILs: THE NEW LEADERS BREAKING THE GLASS CEILING

Being emotionally intelligent is now a "must have" within most leaders. We have all seen global and political leaders around the world lack these essential skills and it drives us crazy! Why? Because when you become more emotionally intelligent you begin to see ignorance and unconscious patterns and behaviors shine through and it can frustrate you immensely.

Just because someone is in a leadership position does not mean that they are in fact, emotionally intelligent, sometimes they're not. However, the world is now calling for both conscious vision and emotionally intelligence within our leaders, and this is a gamechanger.

The younger generations are demanding more from their leaders and rightly so. As a humanity, we are becoming more environmentally aware, more conscious of things like sexism, racism, abuses of power and corruption and more interested in equality, human rights and taking care of our planet.

In a nutshell, we demand more from our leaders. We demand that they are both conscious of the world situation and also emotionally intelligent in how to deal with it, how to make the right decisions and work on behalf on their communities and countries. I believe this demand is both necessary and long overdue. And this is the reason I have developed a new style of leadership, one that doesn't come with the position you hold within a company but one that makes you grow in the areas the world needs.

I call these types of leaders CEILs (sounding like Seals). They are **Conscious, Emotionally Intelligent Leaders**. They are like the Navy Seals of leadership: elite specialists at the top of their chosen field. The word CEIL is also indicative of "breaking the glass ceiling"—a common business term that reflects an invisible barrier to professional advancement often associated with minority groups or discrimination. Many leaders break those glass ceilings and in doing so break new ground in business and life.

I like to see CEILs break glass leadership ceilings and create a new style of leadership: Conscious and Emotionally Intelligent Leadership in all its glory. I think breaking the ceiling of what constitutes leadership is much needed as we evolve and develop.

Let me give you an example. When New Zealand Prime Minister Jacinda Ardern had to face the horrific situation of a brutal massacre in the city of Christchurch she shone a light of the true meaning of conscious emotionally intelligent leadership.

The massacre was a targeted anti-Muslim attack which left 50 innocent people slaughtered. Their crime? Praying peacefully together at a mosque. Ardern flew straight to Christchurch, donned a hijab and hugged and grieved with the bereaved, consoling them with love and compassion.

She demanded questions from the intelligence agencies about why they didn't know about this criminal and she spoke with strength to the public, telling them with conviction that the gun laws will change. When President Trump called her and asked if there was anything he could do to support her and her country, she asked him for love and sympathy toward the Muslim community.

She went on to address this horrific massacre not only with words and understanding but with action and conscious leadership.

She's a CEIL. She is an inspiration.

## WHY CEILs IN THE WORKPLACE ARE KEY

Conscious Emotionally Intelligent Leaders (CEILs) create emotionally intelligent workplaces and teams. In turn, emotionally intelligent work groups achieve positive performance outcomes benefitting each individual and the organization. This means more joy, more money, more awareness and better productivity. Now who doesn't want that?

A CEIL creates:
- a positive workplace environment by promoting positive emotions and practices
- creates trust between work group members
- increases the capacity of workers and work groups to be flexible
- generates ideas and innovation
- increases productivity to reach desired workplace outcomes

- the ability to be flexible and adaptable to change
- looks at work group job satisfaction and motivation
- decreases workplace stress and conflict
- promotes growth of work groups
- promotes personal and professional growth
- advocates equality and inclusion
- creates a safe culture for all ages, cultures and genders
- leads by example

Emotionally intelligent leaders understand the strengths and weaknesses of their team. They invest in training and education and build the culture of the organization. CEILs encourage teams and individuals in their skills, livelihood, abilities and emotional intelligence.

In a study published in the *Journal of Vocational Behavior* by Professor Joseph C. Rode and his colleagues at the Farmer School of Business at Miami University of Ohio, it was found that emotional intelligence is linked to higher salaries and increased job satisfaction.[10] Yes, you and your team can all be happy, successful and emotionally intelligent all at once.

> A research study conducted by Korn Ferry Hay found that 92% of leaders showing a high level of emotional self-awareness had **teams with high energy and high performance.**

## CEILs HAVE GREAT SOCIAL AWARENESS

People with excellent social awareness have greater success in business and life. Did you know that a 40-year study of PhDs at UC Berkeley found that EQ was 400% more powerful than IQ when predicting who would have success in their field.[11]

Social awareness includes attributes such as empathy and understanding team culture and dynamics. Some things are innate to some but need to be learned by others. For example, **empathy isn't a given, sometimes**

**you have to foster it**. A study of nearly 14,000 college students found that students today have about 40% less empathy than college kids had in the 1980s and 1990s.[12] So be mindful that some Millennials or Gen X employees may need to be taught empathy and shown how to cultivate it in the workplace. You can't expect people to have certain attributes that you find desirable or have naturally.

A research team at Cornell University's School of Industrial and Labor Relations explored "What Predicts Executive Success?" as part of a study for the organizational consulting firm Green Peak Partners. They discovered that old-fashioned "my way or the highway" type leadership styles hurt productivity and profit, while self-aware leaders with social EQ always delivered better results.

## EMOTIONS VERSUS MOODS

CEILs are often more socially aware in the workplace and keenly observe others and understand their emotions. They have a "sixth sense" and an acute perception about how to best deal with others, and can feel power shifts or conflicts within groups quite easily.

Doing this to a high degree allows us to distinguish between emotions and moods.

As stated earlier emotions are strong feelings. Moods are a more general or temporary state of mind. The difference between an emotion and a mood is that emotions are capable of disrupting your thought processes whereas a mood is lingering in the background. Moods are sometimes referred to as an emotional state.

Another distinction between emotions and moods is emotions are usually caused by people or situations and often pass quickly. Examples of positive emotions include excitement, pride, being happy and examples of negative emotions include anger, fear and stress. In contrast, moods are usually a personal individual state where the cause of the mood is often not obvious to other people. They can last a long time, over days or even weeks and can be both positive and negative and are not always expressed externally.

To be socially aware it is important to be able to distinguish between emotions and moods. Some sources of moods or emotional states include: stress, feedback from bosses, workplace relationships, conflict, weather, personal matters, personality and cultural factors.

For example, once I was working within a team and I noticed a young woman wasn't being quite herself of late. She was usually quite bubbly and happy to engage in group meetings and conversations at the water cooler. But over the weeks I could feel an energy shift from her. She wasn't as forthcoming in meetings and seemed less emotionally engaged with her work. It was subtle but I noticed it.

One day after work I ran to catch up with her walking to her car. I stopped and asked her if everything was okay, I mentioned how I had noticed she seemed a bit flat lately. It was a small opening but a sincere one. She instantly burst into tears and told me that one of our more senior work colleagues was making her feel inadequate and kept making comments to the boss about any mistakes she had made. It was causing her huge emotional distress but she was trying to operate at work without showing everyone else what was happening.

Being observant to mood or emotional changes within the group is vital for everyone within the group and helps you establish a safe workplace and a positive work culture.

## EMOTION AND CULTURE

Every culture has its own ways of expressing their emotions. As a leader, you should never assume that specific expressions are culturally neutral and carry the same meaning. For example in some cultures pointing your finger at someone is very disrespectful. In fact, some cultures don't express their emotions outwardly at all. This can make building trust more of a challenge however being mindful and respectful of cultural communication differences should be a priority.

You need to use your emotional intelligence to identify, understand and react to cultural differences within your workplace. This will involve becoming familiar with the various emotional cues and emotional states of each diverse individual.

Different cultures express their emotions differently even though they generally have the same range of emotions.

Some key emotional differences among cultures include:
- Prioritization of emotions
- Nonverbal cues
- Freedom of expression

Different cultures prioritize emotions in different ways. Some cultures express anger as a means of releasing the anger and moving on. In Australia and other places like China or Japan for example, it is not acceptable to fully express anger in the workplace.

In Australia we often gesture a "thumbs-up" as a sign of "I'm okay" or "great" whereas in another country this could be a gesture of rudeness. A person from Iran would find it very offensive.

Being ignorant to such things can lead to misunderstandings and potential conflict.

In Japan, sharing ideas in business is often done in a soft and gentle way: allowing others to speak and being considerate of making room for listening and talking. In European or Western countries, business ideas are often loud and boisterous affairs: people talking over one another and raising their voices in excitement or opinion.

In cultures such as Australia, North American and Europe, individuality is celebrated as well as freedom of expression. People are encouraged to speak up, be individual, give feedback and treat each other the same regardless of their position in the workplace. Other cultures, including Portugal, India and Japan are more reserved. In India for example, many areas still have big divisions between people in caste systems or social classes and these can impact some workplaces. Indigenous Australians use minimal eye-contact as a sign of respect, this has often been misinterpreted by foreign people as disrespectful for not making eye-contact.

Lacking in social etiquette or awareness around such matters can result in personal and business disaster.

You should always be looking out for and identifying emotional cues in your work group so you can respond appropriately and in a timely manner. Cues can be verbal or non-verbal. Non-verbal cues include body language, eye contact and gestures. Often these have a different meaning in different cultures. A gesture might be acceptable in your culture but it may be utterly unacceptable or even rude in another.

Learn to engage with your team's individual cultures, ask about their family, get to know their signals and personal nuances.

## PICKING UP ON EMOTIONAL CUES

Emotional cues are any communication that makes you think you should do something. Non-verbal emotional cues give you an idea of what others are feeling or thinking which may be different to the actual words they speak i.e., a work colleague might be telling you they will meet the deadline but at the same time is showing signs of anxiety or nervousness. This may give you a hint they are worried about meeting the deadline.

Non-verbal emotional clues can be:
- **Body language** refers to the movement, stance and gesturing of your body. It can tell you something about a person's emotional state i.e., an upright posture and an open stance with hands visible can indicate confidence while slouching with arms crossed can signal low self-esteem.
- **Facial expressions** are important as it gives you an idea as to what that person is feeling i.e., you can tell if someone is fully engaged in a conversation as normally they usually keep firm eye contact, often nod and occasionally respond verbally. However, in some cultures not looking someone in the eyes is a sign of respect.
- **Paralanguage** refers to non-verbal speech such as tone of voice, pitch, volume and pace. The real message is often not the words they say but how they say them i.e., when calm and relaxed most people talk at an even pace and average volume, however, when someone becomes excited or angry the volume and/or pace usually increases.

Most workplaces today operate in a global business market and as a leader you need to learn emotional cues from diverse cultures within the workplace, including the way you communicate and respond to cultural expressions of emotion.

There are four key adjustments you can make:
1. **Adjusting your interpersonal communication** to suit cultural needs is important for making sure your message is received and understood correctly. This can mean speaking slower using plain English, free from jargon and colloquialisms. Using your emotional intelligence to perceive the level of language competency is important to make sure you don't come across as patronising or condescending. If your work group is culturally diverse, you might also provide important messages in written form as well as verbal to make sure those who do not comprehend speech as well have an accurate account of your communication.

2. **Use social awareness techniques** to connect with culturally diverse work members, clients and customers. The below techniques will help you do this effectively:
   » Regularly check in with individual workers
   » Build trust and confidence
   » Focus your time on those who need it
   » Listen and observe emotional cues
   » Connect work members with appropriate networks
   » Remain open and available for advice and support
   » Operate with honesty and integrity

3. **Build a cultural intelligence culture**
   As a leader of a work group, make sure your workers develop their cultural intelligence through you leading by example and offering training, guidance and support on handling diversity in the workplace. Foster an environment of empathy, patience and

tolerance of cultural differences, and celebrate the value that these differences bring to the workplace. You can:
- » suggest your work group members share their cultural rituals with each other to expand their education and build awareness. Have "Harmony Day" at work where everyone brings a plate of traditional cuisine from their culture and everyone shares it.
- » Offer flexible arrangements that can help to break down cultural barriers i.e., a team member who needs some time off for a cultural celebration such the Lunar New Year, Diwali, Ramadan and NAIDOC Week and can make up the time a different way.

Flexible work practices help support workers to balance work-life commitments and lead to significant workplace benefits including attracting and keeping quality workers. Examples of workplace arrangements include:
- » Flexi working arrangements such as three days in the office, two days' work from home (WFH).
- » Work from home (WFH)
- » Job sharing—two employees share the same role, both in a part time capacity i.e. One person works Monday, Tuesday, Wednesday and the other works Thursday and Friday.
- » Flexi-hours arrangements
- » Overtime/time in lieu
- » Leave options i.e., education leave, carer leave, compassionate leave, etc.
- » Providing childcare services

4. **Respect workplace requirements**
    Your workplace should have policies and procedures in place to support the building of a diverse workforce because a diverse workplace can be a more productive and happy environment. It is however important to make sure diversity aligns with and respects workplace requirements. For example, a fast-paced workplace that delivers products and has strict timelines employing individuals

from cultures where time keeping is not a priority would need to provide training to make sure these workplace needs are met.

Emotional states within groups are really important to promote a good culture and increase positive vibes that will ripple through the workplace. A CEIL responds to the emotional cues and states of others through:
» Spending time to understand their needs
» Giving constructive feedback
» Giving emotional support and guidance
» Respecting individual and cultural differences
» Letting individual workers choose how they would like to complete their work
» Praising good work
» Encouraging workers
» Motivating workers
» Being flexible and adaptable when approaching problem-solving and decision-making
» Valuing and rewarding individual workers contributions
» Providing training and resources if required

A CEIL is a person that sees the individuals within the whole and provides for both.

> Initiative One™ found that workers are 400% less likely to leave a job if they have a high EQ manager. [13]

One person I know who demonstrates all these capacities and operates at the level of CEIL is Dr Mafhav Narayan Sathe, Jt Hon Secretary of The Bombay Mothers and Children Welfare Society (BMCWS). The BMCWS is a charitable Trust with a notable history going back to its founding in 1919. However by 1985 it was struggling to survive through its own financial difficulties.

As a well-respected anaesthetist, Dr Sathe was urged to take the reigns to try and reverse the predicament of the venerated not-for-profit Trust. Through his commitment, acuity and social consciousness he turned the BMCWS into a progressive and sustainable social enterprise that has been making incredible social impacts in rural India for many years now.

I had the honor of talking to Dr Sathe as he reflected on his own influential mentors and the most important quality that has helped him lead the Trust to such lasting change. His altruism is no surprise when you learn of his pioneering relatives who he admires for breaking generational glass-ceilings. I was lucky enough to interview him and ask him about leadership and emotional intelligence.

## MAN ON A MISSION
### AN INTERVIEW WITH DR SATHE (JT HON SECRETARY OF BMCWS)

*My role models were my grandfather and my mother. He was a practicing lawyer while my mother was [only] a 7 standard pass when she was married. This was in 1945, not a year when girls were educated. My grandfather showed courage to educate her and send her to school. He said to her, "I am putting you into the school, but under that pretext, you should not take a refusal and not do your household duties. I should not hear a complaint that you are not working in the house. If that is acceptable to you, then I will put you into school." So my mother started getting up at 4 o'clock in the morning to finish her work and then go to school, come back to finish her studies, finish her work again and then go back to sleep.*

*My mother passed her 12 Standards and my grandfather said, "Do you want to educate further? I will make you a doctor." He put her into medical school and my mother became a doctor. He said, "If you become a doctor, you have to work with the community."*

*She started her practice in 1952; she was the first doctor in my village, a lady doctor! She practiced until 2014. She's 91 years old now.*

Dr Sathe admits he was reluctant to take on the responsibility of BMCWS at first. There were tremendous expectations of taking on the reputation of this well-known organization as well as the more pragmatic headaches of unravelling the, "…basket of problems," within the organization. He reflected on his initial reluctance:

*Suddenly there was a question that came to mind: what are you scared of? What will happen if you take it? I was scared of a defeat, of losing. Then I asked myself how to deal with this situation if it happened? The only answer was to face it, to accept it. What did that mean? To make way for another person to come in and take over. Don't allow your pride to make the organization lose. This was not difficult for me because I was a player: cricket, badminton on big district and state levels. If you lose, forget it and say okay I lost, let somebody else work on it but your organization will survive.*

Knowing that he could overcome his fear should he fail, Dr Sathe rose to the challenge as he realized:

*I could serve many people if I accepted this challenge. I didn't have any experience in administration, finances, economics, accounting, human resources—nothing. But I have logic. Besides my medical knowledge, what I realized coming over here is that you need to understand all the nitty gritties of the organization with simple logic. All those areas are logical things. If you have logic, you can know how to handle things…I tackled the Union problem, the labor problem. I did a lot of innovations. Getting a donor for everything was not possible. So I wanted to have my own money at my own disposal to change the organization gradually without the outside source. Logical thinking was the answer to everything.*

Dr Sathe was able to apply modern business models to overhaul the *not-for-profit* mentality to one of *not-for-loss*, convincing corporate investors and stake-holders of the long-term benefits in small, short-term loans which, over time, created channels of income that could be rolled back into their social welfare programs. The BMCWS became a ground-breaking sustainable social enterprise.

I was captured by the importance Dr Sathe put on logic to successfully communicate across so many stakeholders, investors, staff and villagers. I asked him if it was something people are born with.

*You are born with it but you have to have a playing field for it to blossom. Some of it comes to you in parenting, some in student life, some from leading the sports teams and becoming captain of the team. As captain you have to be very logical and understanding, about your opponent's strengths and weaknesses and your strengths and weaknesses. I was also the leader of the student union but I was never an activist in that sense, the argument, the fighting no. I was always a constructive critic of a system. Now I have a big playing field to use [logic] and for it to blossom.*

Dr Sathe's sees his social consciousness as a kind of duty considering the very limited facilities, resources and technology that reach rural people in India.

*I feel that somewhere, I have taken up something which otherwise would have gone to them. Being the city person, we have all the facilities. Rural people even today don't have the water, the roads, the electricity. I feel that I am partly responsible for not allowing this to reach them. It is not doing anything "more," this should have gone back as their right. I don't have the slightest "great feeling" that I am being a "great help" to the people. It is my duty. They are a deprived community because we in the city and the government haven't given enough to them. It is not help. Once you call it help and start walking two inches above the ground [as if] "I am doing it for you," that is a bad feeling to tell anybody. So if you want yourself to be grounded, you have to be thinking that it is something which ought to be done. I am only a mediator.*

It is with such compassion and understanding that Dr Sathe has managed to forge strong, mutually respectful relationships between the corporate, government and charitable sectors that are making admirable achievements in the health and education of rural villages.

There may be linguistic differences in the way it's described, however logic is a huge component of emotional intelligence because it discerns how a goal can be achieved from a place of great compassion and consideration for all parties involved. As Dr Sathe explained so beautifully, it is something we are born with but also something that must be nurtured.

It is my hope that other people will follow Dr Sathe's approach and use logic coupled with emotional intelligence to help make the world a better place.

## IS IT NATURAL OR NURTURED?

Some people are instinctively emotionally intelligent; through life's curveballs and challenges they may have developed their emotional intelligence at an early age. While for others it may be a learned behavior, a result of increased learning through their career and education courses. Others may have wrestled with emotional self-regulation and conflict and developed it out of the need to better understand themselves and others. Some people don't have emotional intelligence and are oblivious to the social implications of not having it. Some grossly over-estimate their level of emotional intelligence. For example, a 2016 study published in *Personality and Mental Health* revealed that narcissists consistently overestimated their emotional intelligence.[14]

It seems that in most cases, EQ can be both natural and nurtured.

A CEIL can look at the bigger picture and understand that everyone should have access to these abilities and in doing so can develop them with the right support, encouragement and awareness. Many business places are now adding this type of training into their workplace.

A CEIL has a wide-range of awareness about personal and global matters, and he or she also does their best to awaken them in others. It's the mark of true conscious citizenship and morality in areas such as:

**Social Intelligence**
The ability to understand and integrate social relationships, partnerships, group dynamics and individuals.

**Multi-Cultural Intelligence**
The ability to understand, communicate, respect and empathize with other cultures and indigenous communities.

**Generational Intelligence**
The ability to understand, communicate, respect and empathize with diverse generations and their needs into society and the workplace.

**Inclusion and Integration Intelligence**
The ability to understand, communicate, respect and empathize with diverse sectors of any race, gender, sexual orientation, ability or disability and religion and include and integrate their needs into society and the workplace.

**Global Intelligence**
The ability to understand global matters and crises and respond with a high level of emotional intelligence for communities, countries and individuals.

Acting as a role model encourages and supports positive emotions and discourages negative emotions. Yes, time and time again Emotional Intelligence is the silent partner behind someone's success. TalentSmart tested emotional intelligence alongside 33 other important and necessary workplace skills, and found that EQ is the strongest predictor of performance! It's not just about your technical skillset anymore, sure they are equally important but they aren't the only thing.

## BEING A CEIL IS THE NEW BENCHMARK

If you're not convinced by the need to increase your capacity for conscious and emotionally intelligent leadership, then you may not seamlessly move forward into the new world that demands an increase in this awareness.

Jacinda Ardern's and Dr Mafhav Narayan Sathe examples of leadership that we touched on in this chapter should not be as rare as they are. Imagine the world if we actively voted and cultivated CEILs all through the different sectors and industries. No industry should be left behind.

If anything, we need all systems, all industries, all business and political sectors, along with educational and health sectors to cultivate CEILs. A full global system of conscious leaders!

---

*"Knowing what must be done does away with fear."*
**Rosa Parks**

---

## CHAPTER 3

# LEAD WITH PURPOSE

### PURPOSE HELPS YOU LIVE YOUR VALUES

*"When we live our purpose, we lead a life worth living."*
**Catherine Molloy**

If you consider yourself a leader, then you know that leadership starts from the time you wake up in the morning until the time your head hits the pillow at night. Leadership is part of your purpose, part of your reason for being. By harnessing the tools in this book, leadership becomes easier. However, the minute you become complacent, progress can slip, and the wheels can begin to fall off.

Leadership is a purpose-driven ability that you can hone and strengthen every single day. So, I say, "Do leadership on purpose." True leadership leaves a legacy in the way that you live, and at the heart of this is purpose.

It takes a purpose driven CEIL to lead with truly inspired action and to harness a culture and purpose that outlives the organization. An organization's culture can be destroyed without purpose, values, and strong leadership.

As I travel the world talking with groups and meeting many people, I often get asked, "But Cath, how do I know what my purpose is?" Of course, there are countless products, courses, and workshops on this exact topic, but I think it can be summed up very quickly with one question and one answer.

*Q: What is your purpose?*
*A: Your purpose is what gets you up in the morning.*

As bestselling author and philosopher Bob Proctor said, "Your purpose explains what you are doing with your life. Your vision explains how you are living your purpose. Your goals enable you to realize your vision."

We are going to look at all three of the these in this chapter: vision, goals, and purpose.

*What gets you up and out of bed?* Take a minute to ask yourself that question. Why do you do what you do? What ignites you to get up? If you're not inspired to get up and out of bed, then what would make you excited to wake up every day? How would you use your time?

Identifying your purpose is often coupled with passion. It's what your soul calls you to do. For some, it's to create a business, a piece of art, or a book. For others, it may be to collaborate with business partners on new projects or to help someone else. There are no rules to what fills you with bliss.

What gets me up and out of bed may be very different to what gets you up and out of bed. It must be more than just your morning coffee that gives you the desire to get up. But coffee helps too!

For me, I love to make a difference in people's lives; it gets me all geared up and ready to meet the day, full of energy. For example, I have worked with a lot of teenagers through a government incentive program that selects 150 candidates and puts them through one of our programs. Some of these teens have mental health issues and feel a lack of purpose in their lives. I have loved seeing the change in them as they have progressed through developing new body language and communication skills, and the confidence that ensues. We have helped them to learn and practice their new skills and to refine old ones—like how to shake hands and how to communicate and read body language. Often, by the third day of these courses, there is a notable difference in the students. They start taking more responsibility for themselves, they become more openly caring to the person beside them (who they did not like at the beginning), and they look at people more equally, regardless of color, race, or age. From being closed, they begin to open up and say hi to others, helping them or chatting with them.

The results from these courses have been phenomenal. One young lady, Kate, did not think there was any reason to live. She had attempted suicide a few times. She was taking part in the course out of a sense of obligation to her mother more than anything else. By the end of the program, Kate was a different person. She found out that she was good at many things and had a future worth fighting for. Now, Kate has completed a nursing degree and is working fulltime as a nurse.

That's why I get up every day.

Another young lady who completed our course, Sara, was immediately employed in hospitality three days a week, before picking up an additional job, which allowed her to move out of the rental she was sharing with seven other people (who were bad influences on her anyway). She was so proud to be able to rent her own apartment and now has a great relationship with her mum, is building a relationship with her dad, and still holds the same jobs two years later. Sara found a purpose in life, continued to set her goals, and started to move in a direction she felt excited by.

The path is much harder if you do not have any goals to work towards. For that young lady to build a better relationship with her mum and dad, she created a lot of mini goals to get away from the people around her who took drugs. She reduced her circle to three close friends who she knew didn't drink or take drugs. Sara turned her whole life around because she really understood every domino effect that came from her actions, reactions, or even lack of action. Now she is leading herself and leading a life she deems worth living!

That's worth getting up for, right?

Helping people to create a better life fills my life. It's a win–win situation. As the old adage says, 'If you do what you love, you never work a day in your life.'

## GOING BEYOND YOURSELF

When my husband, John, fell ill, and we lost one million dollars, I really wanted to regain what we had lost. I realized that I had to reinvent my life right there and then, so I dug deep to find out what I really wanted to do for the rest of my life. I decided to make the goal bigger than myself and give 10% of everything I earned to charity. When I told John, he asked why I would do that—we had lost nearly everything, and I had not made any money yet, so why would I choose to give it away? I said that I needed the goal to be bigger than us. In other words, I needed a purpose that exceeded my own survival.

Good mental wealth comes from helping others. Helping somebody else helps to create a purpose for getting up in the morning. You might learn a new skill, such as sewing, and start sewing items for people in need (masks) or for injured wildlife (pouches), or you might help to build fences and create shelters for farms, as John and I did after the 2019/20 bushfires. There are a lot of different causes to choose from; you just have to start looking.

In many ways, making the cause bigger than myself is how I came to write *The Million Dollar Handshake*. I was successfully running training programs and speaking with a full schedule. I kept being asked to put my knowledge into a book, but I was hesitant. I didn't have the time, yet I understood the power of knowledge. The decision to write the book came about by setting a goal to sell one million copies, with one third of the proceeds of all books sold being donated to charity. I realized that if I sold a million copies, it would lighten my own fundraising burden. Sometimes, even with the purpose of helping others, I felt weighed down because I didn't have time to do the fundraising I needed to do while running a company and traveling overseas. By making the cause bigger than myself, I had a goal. It helped me to establish purpose, which drove me to write my first book.

Purpose is a driving force that takes the obligation out of work. Working with purpose is beyond our old description of work. We don't work just for a paycheck. We work to give our lives meaning and purpose beyond money. Don't get me wrong, we all need and want money to live. It's the global currency of exchange. But we are not all working solely for money these days. Many of us feel that inner drive to go beyond money and to make work mean something more than an exchange of labor for cash. Simon Sinek has become a well-known voice for being purpose driven in a profit-driven world. He said, "Profit isn't a purpose. It's a result. To have purpose means the things we do are of real value to others."[1]

I couldn't agree more. Profit is a result and results are fantastic, but results are the effect of the value that we give.

A recent study by multi-national PricewaterhouseCoopers (PwC) shows that a whopping 79% of business leaders surveyed said that a company's purpose is central to its business success.[2] However, it also revealed that 68% said that purpose is not used in leadership decision-making processes within their company. Isn't that fascinating? The vast majority agree that purpose is the cornerstone of business success, but not all leaders were basing their decisions around that value.

The 2016 PwC report "Putting Purpose to Work: A Study of Purpose in the Workplace" also said that millennials with a strong connection to a company's purpose are 5.3 times more likely to stay. That being said, only 33% of employees draw any real meaning from their employer's purpose.[3] I believe this highlights a massive need for both employees and employers to work on the company's purpose, mission, and vision together, so that they feel a deep sense of connection with it. It shouldn't be something that the CEO or founder comes up with and expects everyone to feel connected with. It needs a mutual sense of belonging to be successful long term. In fact, employees who derive meaning from their work have almost twice the level of job satisfaction than those who don't derive meaning, and are three times more likely to stay with the company.[4]

Of course, it's not only employees that crave purpose-driven companies to work for. Customers also want to give their hard-earned money to purpose-driven businesses. Edelman's "Good Purpose" report shows:

- 90% of consumers would blacklist a brand if they discovered irresponsible business practices (and more than 55% have done just that within the past twelve months).
- 91% of consumers would switch brands to support a brand of similar quality and price if that brand supported a good cause.[5]

Leading-edge experts on purpose, Cone and Porter Novelli, show that customers view purpose-driven brands as being more caring. As a result, customers are more loyal to them for their caring culture than to brands that don't show a purpose-driven message.[6]

Purpose and meaning aren't just a bonus you get with a good company or brand; they are now becoming critical to long-term business success. People are demanding that they buy from businesses with purpose, and employees are seeking to give their time, effort, and energy to businesses with a high degree of ethics and purpose. Dismiss these findings at your peril.

When you work for something beyond profit, you are inspired by something larger than your bank account. The ancient Indian sage Patanjali remarked, "When you are inspired by some great purpose, some extraordinary project, all your thoughts break their bonds. Your mind transcends limitations, your consciousness expands in every direction, and you find yourself in a new, great and wonderful world. Dormant forces, faculties and talents become alive, and you discover yourself to be a greater person, far greater than you ever dreamed yourself to be."[7]

I have also felt this dormant force come alive inside me.

One day, I met a lady who was running a Shine program for one of the state schools in our area. It was a program specifically helping young women who had been bullied, abused, or came from broken homes. I was fortunate in that she asked if I would come and help. It was a ten-week program about unlocking your value and worth. Through working with this lady, I discovered that she and some of her friends from a local church group were looking after orphans in Uganda, and I started fundraising with them. After a few years, they asked me to come with them to Uganda. It was a life-changing experience. My world instantly grew larger, as did my heart. These beautiful, innocent orphans gave me more than I gave them. They gave me deeper compassion, greater empathy, and a determination to help as many of them as I can. I have been back more than once. I took my daughter with me on one trip and my husband on another. Now, 10% of everything I earn goes to charities that support orphans, both in Uganda and India. This fills me with purpose. Patanjali is right: when there is something bigger than you, dormant forces come alive and all your thoughts break their bonds. You also become happier because purpose is beyond calculating time, money, and effort. It gives you more to live for and allows you to be happy about your contribution.

To be as purposeful as possible, it is important to reflect on the previous chapters—to grow as a CEIL and be conscious of your leadership.

## PURPOSEFUL MINDS

Purpose often springs from a heightened sense of emotional intelligence and conscious awareness.

Stanford University researcher and psychologist Carol Dweck changed the landscape of mindset and learning when she showed us the two types of mindsets that affect our outcomes and learning attitudes: the "growth mindset" and the "fixed mindset."

Over 30 years ago, Carol Dweck became interested in learning attitudes about failure. She noticed that some students bounced back quickly from perceived failures, while others got upset by small setbacks. Why did some develop resilience and others did not?

Over time, Dweck realized that many individuals have underlying beliefs and views of where their abilities come from. She coined the terms fixed mindset and growth mindset based on these findings to describe the underlying beliefs that people have about learning and intelligence.[8]

To cut a long study short, the crux of the findings was that people with a growth mindset believe that their success is based on hard work, learning, and training. They know that they can adapt, change, and turn something from a weakness into a strength. They understand that all skills can be learned and developed with time and effort. However, people with a fixed mindset believe that their success is based on their innate ability, which is limited. They believe that when it comes to your skillset or abilities, you either have it or you don't.

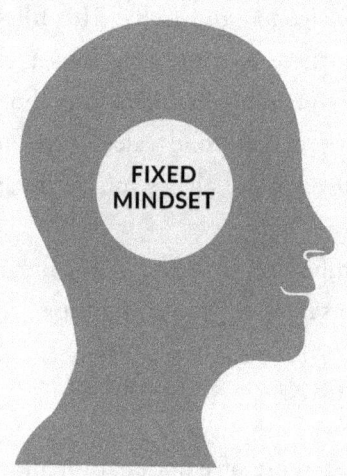 

**Fixed Mindset**

*"My intelligence is fixed and won't change."*

*"I am either good or natural at something or I'm not."*

*"I take criticism personally."*

*"It's difficult to improve."*

*"There's no point in even trying."*

*"I'm really not good at this."*

**Growth Mindset**

*"I can improve if I keep trying."*

*"Other people's successes inspire me."*

*"Mistakes help me learn and grow."*

*"I learn a lot from challenges."*

*"Feedback is valuable and makes me better."*

*"I can learn anything if I put my mind to it."*

Adapted from the work of Carol Dweck

Many people assume that a growth mindset is simply being open-minded but it's much more than that. It's not magical thinking. It is the ability to handle setbacks and develop resilience in a way that allows room for positive growth and new development. It means that your skills and abilities are not fixed but are able to flourish with the right know-how and training.

This is especially important when it comes to purpose and goals. Purpose is not something you instantly know at birth (unless you are the Dalai Lama of course); it is something that often gets developed over time and honed as you age. It can be fluid and changing as you go through life, much like your goals. You do not have the same goals now that you had when you were ten. We change our goals in accordance with our dreams and values, and these often mature and change over time.

So, though this chapter is based on purpose, goals, and visualization, it's important to view these with a growth mindset. See them as being able to be learned and developed over time by taking some actions and adding effort.

## MAKE A PURPOSE STATEMENT

To keep a growth mindset around purpose, it can be helpful to make and adopt a purpose statement. This keeps your purpose at the forefront of your mind and behavior. Many people get confused by purpose statements and wonder how they differ from mission statements. However, the distinction is simple. A mission statement is what you do, and a purpose statements is why you do it.

| Mission – What we do | Purpose – Why we do it |
|---|---|
| Running a business | Making a difference |
| Creating a profit | To support people financially |
| Develop workshops | To inspire and educate leaders |
| Produce products | To leave a legacy |

| Teach leadership | To increase consciousness |
|---|---|
| Grow a business | Build a community |

Here is an example of how to craft your purpose statement.

## PURPOSE STATEMENT TEMPLATE

**The purpose of the** _____
(name of service, program or line of business)

**is to provide (or produce)** _____
(service or product - what)

**for** _____
(customer - who)

**so that** _____
(result/benefit - why)

The co-founder of Hewlett-Packard, David Packard, voiced his definition of purpose in a 1960 speech to a training group.

> *I want to discuss why a company exists in the first place. In other words, why are we here? I think many people assume, wrongly, that a company exists simply to make money. While this is an important result of a company's existence, we have to go deeper and find the real reasons for our being... Purpose (which should last at least 100 years) should not be confused with specific goals or business strategies (which should change many times in 100 years). Whereas you might achieve a goal or complete a strategy, you cannot fulfill a purpose; it is like a guiding star on the horizon—*

*forever pursued but never reached. Yet although purpose itself does not change; it does inspire change. The very fact that purpose can never be fully realized means that an organization can never stop stimulating change and progress.*[9]

Some great examples from other companies are:
- NASA's purpose is to "reach for new heights and reveal the unknown for the benefit of humankind."
- Patagonia: "We're in business to save our home planet."
- Lego does not just sell kids' toys; they exist to aid "the development of children's creativity through play and learning."

These statements have purpose and do what David Packard describes. They reach far into the future, well beyond business goals and KPIs.

The CEO of BlackRock, Larry Fink, is passionate about purpose. In 2018, he wrote an open letter to CEOs called, "A Sense of Purpose."[10] It made many CEOs stand up and take notice. In 2019, he followed it up with another bold letter entitled, "Purpose & Profit." He wrote:

*As I have written in past letters, a company cannot achieve long-term profits without embracing purpose and considering the needs of a broad range of stakeholders. A pharmaceutical company that hikes prices ruthlessly, a mining company that short-changes safety, a bank that fails to respect its clients—these companies may maximize returns in the short term. But, as we have seen again and again, these actions that damage society will catch up with a company and destroy shareholder value. By contrast, a strong sense of purpose and a commitment to stakeholders helps a company connect more deeply to its customers and adjust to the changing demands of society. Ultimately, purpose is the engine of long-term profitability.*[11]

Purposeful leadership is all about being willing to help others see the long game, the deep "why" that exists within business.

## EFFECTIVE PURPOSEFUL LEADERSHIP

A leader with purpose ignites the sense of purpose within others. Sir Richard Branson is a great example of a purposeful leader. He allows his people to lead from the front and provides them with more than just a job. Branson built a team that echoes his participative leadership. He utilizes other people's strengths and hires his weaknesses. He likes to promote from within, building a culture where continual passion for the job and demonstrations of leadership skill are rewarded with leadership roles. In other words, he encourages purposeful leadership within his organization.

"Leadership doesn't have a secret formula; all true leaders go about things in their own way," says Branson. "What leadership boils down to, is people. Whatever your style, whatever your method, you need to believe in yourself, your ideas and your staff. Nobody can be successful alone, and you cannot be a great leader without great people to lead."[12]

An effective, purposeful leader has all the qualities of being a CEIL and ignites these qualities within others. He or she arms others to see purpose as a continuing ambition with no finish line. Purpose is the inner driving force behind the goals, strategies, systems, and methods employed by the organization. This is why Simon Sinek's famous book *Start with Why* became a bestseller. The old paradigm of business shifted, and Sinek's book highlighted the deeper purpose that people were desperately seeking within their working environments.

## INEFFECTIVE LEADERSHIP WITH NO PURPOSE

The leader who divides and conquers and does not have or share a greater sense of purpose will find trouble is not too far away. Clients will leave for a more purpose-driven brand, and employees will jump ship to a more purpose-driven employer.

You can give your staff the best of everything, such as open and varied workspaces, breakout lounges, free food, and childcare, but if the company and leader lacks a deeper "why" then the long-term inner sense of meaning isn't fulfilled. Most people want to feel valued and contribute the best of themselves and their skills. If people feel purposeful, they get up every day with a reason that far outweighs just getting through the day.

## VALUE YOUR VALUES

Every organization has its own mission statement and values. As an individual, it is important that you identify which values are important to you and keep them at the forefront of your mind. Knowing your values helps you to know what is important to you. It also allows you to notice whether your own behavior, or someone else's, does not align with your core values. When looking to change jobs, you can check the values of an organization and see if they align with yours before proceeding. You can carry your top three values on your phone, set reminders, or put them up at home (add them to your vision board) where you will see and be reminded of them every day. However, usually you do not need to be reminded of your values at all, because once you discover them, they just feel right inside. They are congruent with your morals, actions, thoughts, and behaviors.

I revisit my values annually, just to check in and see whether anything has changed. Sometimes, the values remain the same but the priority changes. It is important that you understand your values so that you can live true to who you are. If your top value is family, dig down and see what that family value really means to you. How much time do you wish to spend with them? Is it a barbecue together once a week? Is it calling your mum every day or once a week? Is it planning an extended family holiday once a year? After setting your core values, check in throughout the month and see how you are tracking on that value and whether it needs to change.

My top three values are courage, family, and health. When I look at courage, it has always been 100%—I haven't held myself back, I've stepped into everything, and there has been no comfort-zone barrier. However, when it comes to family, my self-rating dropped to 40%. I often focused so much on work and building my business, as the primary income earner, that I realized I had become unconscious around my family. My son was at university and I had forgotten to check in with him. By revisiting my values, I was able to make changes. I now check in regularly by text or pick up the phone to say hi and see how he is doing. I have also added fortnightly family barbecues. Without my annual check in, I may have remained unconscious to my behavior and not realized that my values were not congruent with my actions.

I have seen grown men cry at events because they had missed connecting with their children because they were busy fulfilling the role of provider. It is easy to do small things that can mean a world of difference. One of the values in my business is family. If a team member has a school activity, such as their child presenting or receiving an award at assembly or sports day, they are free to attend these events so that they and their children do not miss out.

My third value was equally in need of attention. I also rated myself at 40% for health. While health is important to me, I do not always make it a priority. By revisiting this value, I was able to course-correct and implement actions that prioritize health.

Identifying values is about finding out who you are and what is important to you deep down. Remember that everyone has value. Everyone is one of a kind and everyone is precious. My values may be different to yours, but they are no less valuable.

Knowing your values helps you to understand what drives you—what you enjoy, what inspires you, and what you would like more of. By building a life and lifestyle around our values, you create a life that is more satisfying and meaningful. Values change over time and deepen as you understand yourself better. They are always dynamic. Your values can also be situational. What is true for you at work might not be true for you at home. Your values act as your inner compass in life.

## IDENTIFYING YOUR CORE VALUES

Let us identify your personal core values to help you make decisions that will be in harmony with the values that are important to you.

### STEP 1: SELECT

Identify ten values that are important to you and write them in the boxes below. For ideas, you can view a list of over 200 values in the interactive book. There are no right or wrong values. Go with your instincts and choose the values you feel most strongly about. If your value isn't listed, please add it as one of your values.

## STEP 2: PRIORITIZE AND SCORE

Write your core values in order of importance to you, from one to ten. Write a percentage value (0%–100%) next to each value, which reflects how you are living that value right now, e.g., family 40%.

| Value | Percentage |
| --- | --- |
| 1. | |
| 2. | |
| 3. | |
| 4. | |
| 5. | |
| 6. | |
| 7. | |
| 8. | |
| 9. | |
| 10. | |

## STEP 3: DEFINE AND ACTION

Take your top three values and write down what each value means to you. This exercise helps to clarify what is important to you.

Value one is the value you revert to when all else fails, i.e., the one that has the most meaning in your life right now.

Next, write down two actions you can take for each of your top three values to reach the highest percentage possible, allowing you to live in alignment with your values.

| **Value 1:** |
|---|
| What this value means to me: |
| Action 1: |
| Action 2: |

| **Value 2:** |
|---|
| What this value means to me: |
| Action 1: |
| Action 2: |

| Value 3: |
|---|
| What this value means to me: |
| Action 1: |
| Action 2: |

## STEP 4: COMMIT

Now that you have worked out the actions you need to take to reflect your top three values, it's time to commit to taking these actions daily.

On your smartphone, record your top three values and how you will live into your core self, e.g., "My first core value is…I believe I am currently living to this at…percent. The two actions I need to take to live this value even more are: one, to…, and two, to…"

## VISION BOARDS

Visualization is one of the most powerful mind exercises that you can do. There is endless research into visualization techniques and the powerful impact they have on achieving your goals.

When I was a full-time mother raising three children on one salary from my little home business selling kids clothes, shoes, books, and toys, I had heard that you could attract what you would like in your life and decided to explore this further. I had always wanted to go to Uluru (Ayers Rock), but I had no idea how I could afford to take three children out of school and to Uluru on one salary plus my home job.

I stuck an image of Uluru on my fridge. It acted as a daily reminder and helped me to envisage my dream. I saw it every day and imagined being there with my family. Long story short, we made it to Uluru, and it was amazing! When I returned from that trip, I immediately changed my picture to Paris—I was hooked!

A picture is worth a thousand words. Goal setting and mind-mapping help you to clarify exactly what you would like your life to look like. Using tools such as dream boards filled with words and pictures helps you to visualize the end result, making it more attainable.

Whether it's a holiday, styling or renovating your house, buying a new house, etc., creating a dream board of what you desire in your life allows your body to experience your goals on another level. It allows you to visualize what it looks like for you and feel what it would be like in your body when you achieve it, e.g., joy, excitement, etc. Images are a constant reminder of what it is that you are working towards. You can put it on your fridge, bathroom mirror, or bedroom wall. Create a screensaver for your phone or computer, create a pin board on Pinterest, or cut out pictures and words and stick them onto a piece of cardboard.

# MAKING YOUR OWN VISION BOARD
## PHYSICAL VISION BOARD

**What You Need:** Your imagination! Magazines, scissors, cardboard, and glue.

**Step 1:** Go through your magazines and tear the images from them. No gluing yet! Just let yourself have fun looking through magazines and pulling out pictures, words, or headlines that strike your fancy. Make a big pile of images, phrases, and words. If you cannot find the image you are after, jump online, print them out, and add them to your pile.

**Step 2:** Go through the images and begin to lay your favorites on the board. Eliminate any images that no longer feel right. Follow your intuition. As you place the pictures on the board, you'll get a sense of how the board should be laid out. For instance, you might assign a theme to each corner of the board, e.g., health, job, spirituality, or relationships. You may want the images to go all over the place or you could fold the board into a book that tells a story. At my retreats, I have seen women come up with wildly creative ways to present a dream board.

**Step 3:** Glue everything onto the board. Add writing if you want to. You can paint on it or write words with markers.

**Step 4 (Optional but Powerful):** Leave space in the very center of the vision board for a fantastic photo of yourself, in which you look radiant and happy. Paste that picture in the center of your board.

**Step 5:** Hang your vision board in a place where you will see it often.

## ONLINE VISION BOARD

**What You Need:** Your imagination! A computer.

**Step 1:** Search for images online that represent what you would like your life to look like. You can copy the images and paste them into your preferred program in which you will create your board, e.g., Canva, Publisher, PowerPoint, Google Slides, etc. Make the document A3 size and save your file before you begin! Add a couple of extra pages to the document for dropping in images.

**Step 2:** Make one page a blank page. This will be your board. Go through the images and copy your favorites to the blank page/board. Delete any images that no longer feel right. Follow your intuition. As you place the pictures on the board, you will get a sense of how the board should be laid out.

**Step 3:** Lay your board out and add any words and phrases. Save your document!

**Step 4 (Optional but Powerful):** Find a fantastic photo of yourself, in which you look radiant and happy, and drop it onto the center of your board. Save your document!

**Step 5:** Once laid out, you can download the page, save it as a JPEG file, or take a screenshot and save it to your device. You can upload it as a screensaver or view your board every day before you begin the day. You can even print out the screenshot and hang it where you will see it often.

You can do the same exercise using Pinterest or Trello, saving pins to a vision board and taking a screenshot to grab an image to use.

## MIND-MAPPING

If you are creative and prefer to draw your vision board, you may enjoy a mind-mapping exercise. Mind-mapping can also be used to break down an individual goal, such as a career promotion or a product launch, and the steps required to achieve it.

1. Set your purpose/goal.
2. Turn a blank piece of paper sideways (landscape) and start in the center.
3. Sketch an image of your focus in the center.
4. Use at least three colors for emphasis, structure, texture, and creativity.

5. Draw curved lines radiating from the center (thick to thin) connecting the main branches to the central image and moving outwards to further levels.
6. Use one key word or image per line for more power and flexibility in your thinking.
7. Use images throughout your mind map, as a picture paints a thousand words.

Below is an example of a mind map I created to explore all the things in my life. I could also take one theme from this and mind map it in more detail.

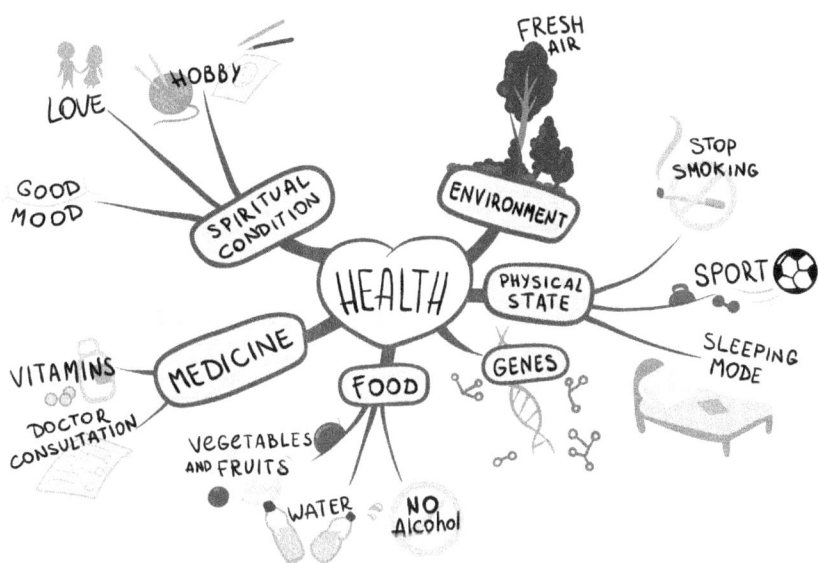

But it's not just me that knows the power of mind-mapping. I'd like to introduce you to René Deceuninck, a worldwide public speaker who has worked alongside and spent personal time with mind-mapping founder and author Tony Buzan, and has also shared the stage with Brian Tracy, Jairek Robbins, Jack Canfield and many other influential speakers. René is also hosting preview sessions for Anthony Robbins' UPW Events.

Today, René still loves setting goals; and together with award-winning entrepreneur, Chrissy Tasker and myself, are creating The Hart Academy for Influencers. This is what René has to say about mind-mapping and goal-setting.

## KEEPING YOUR VISION ON PURPOSE
*AN INTERVIEW WITH RENÉ DECEUNINCK*

I love using mind-maps because I need visuals. For me, mind-mapping is important to help me remain focused on what is important. We all have a brain: a left hemisphere and a right hemisphere, a rational part and an emotional part, and we all have a reticular activating system (RAS) that shows our brain where to focus and where energy flows.

And it reminds me of a story by Dr Wayne Dyer who said it's like when you've been thinking about somebody the whole day—they live on the other side of the country, and you didn't hear from them for five consecutive years. But for some reason, this particular day, you can't stop thinking about them. That same evening, the phone goes and who is on the phone? That person right? Some people say, how strange?! But basically, you can synchronize with a thought, and you can manifest.

When you begin to understand how manifestation works, your life changes.

But first, you have to synchronize with a thought. And how can you synchronize with a thought? You have to have that visual image so that the reticular activating system part of the brain is constantly seeing that visual.

Now, you can put a mind-map in your kitchen, in your bathroom, in your bedroom and on the ceiling, it doesn't matter where you put it, as long as you see it on a constant basis. And when I see my mind-map on a constant basis, my energy goes towards what is on it. For example, when I started my company, I drafted a website, created social media, collected email addresses and I planned all my future books, seminars and webinars. And when I was looking at the website draft, I thought *wow, wouldn't it be great to have that in real life?* My vision was drafted but not yet "real." Your vision is where greatness begins. Nothing happens without a goal, dream or vision.

> *"Nothing happens unless first we dream."*
> **Carl Sandburg**

So what is the first step to success? Research mind-maps and start to learn about them. Get yours going straight away.

When you finish your mind-map, the key to knowing if it's powerful enough is that you look at it and think, *Wow! Isn't that amazing?!* Take a step or two back and look at it again. This map is your helicopter view—a general overview of what you would love to create. I like to leave my mind-map for around three or four days, and go back to it after I'm out of that initial phase of creativity. Then, I take my green marker and make any adjustments to it. I may adjust something or delete something. I always make any alterations in green. So I have my original mind-map with a green one on top of it.

I then take three or four steps backwards and look at my mind-map again, I make any changes in green and leave it again for three-four days.

A few days later, I take the blue marker and start changing, adding, deleting, whatever needs to be done. Then I step back to get my helicopter view and leave it for another three-four days.

Days later, I finalize my mind-map with the red marker.

Now I have a strong mind-map of where I really want to go. Naturally, things will change along the way of course but it's a great beginning, and that RAS in your brain is actively engaging in being the search engine of your dreams.

You will begin to notice and see things on your map. For example. if are driving a Volkswagen but you want to drive a BMW, you go to the BMW dealership and discuss the possibility. The bank okays the loan payments and your new BMW can be delivered in three months. As you walk away from that dealership and drive back home, all of a sudden, you're driving your Volkswagen but seeing your BMW everywhere.

It's super important to have that mind-map visual on your wall before you see it in real life. You must! That's why Einstein said 'Imagination is more important than knowledge.' And that's what I learned from many great leaders.

If you want that brand new Jaguar, take pictures of it and put them everywhere, you will end up driving that car, sooner or later. I dreamt about the Mercedes-Benz S-Class. I love luxury, I don't want to pay for it but I love it. Today I drive one. How? Because I had that picture everywhere. I was dreaming about it. I thought how wonderful it would be to drive one. How incredible the seats would feel. Sometimes people would say, "René, stop talking about your Mercedes, there are other things in life!" I would reply, "I know…but one day I will be driving it." And today I do. The next step is an Aston Martin. My desktop screensaver is an Aston Martin and I look at it every single freaking day. Each time I open the computer group my mind-map is there. And I guarantee you, I will drive one, and I know that it all starts with a mind-map.

It's not just about having "stuff" either. Mind-maps are brilliant for focusing your energy on experiences and things that deeply matter to you. For some, it could be building a charity or volunteering regularly. For others, it could be to meet their idols or travel to a place they have always wanted to go.

When I was 11 years old I received a book from my mom and dad, called Kung Fu. It was filled with Chinese wisdom and quotes from Confucius. Now to be quite honest, I would have preferred a bike not a book, so I put the book away but I was aware there may be a deeper purpose behind the gift. But I was eleven years old all I wanted was a bike.

When I was about 18-19 years old, I picked up the book and saw that it was filled with amazing wisdom, mostly based on the *Tao Te Ching* from the ancient master Lao Tzu. So, I began buying books from authors like the Dalai Lama, Deepak Chopra and Wayne Dyer.

I thought—*wouldn't it be great to meet the Dalai Lama.*

In 2002, my dad died at the age of 78, and before they closed the coffin, during the last reading, I thought—if there's one thing I'm going to do before I die, is I'm going to pursue all my goals and dreams, and one of them is meeting the Dalai Lama.

I went home and started praying and meditating for a while. After a while, I said to myself, *René, stop doing this shit because it's not working. When you are meant to meet him, you will; if you're not meeting him, that's because you're not ready for it. So, keep thinking about it, meditate as much as you want, but don't focus on it.*

I did keep thinking about it but I toned down my hellbent approach, instead I imagined it in a lighter way and even went as far as to imagine meeting him in Belgium. I didn't tell anyone about my secret desire, not even my children.

Four years later, in 2006, on Father's Day, one of my daughters hands me an envelope with two tickets inside to meet the Dalai Lama—in Belgium.

I believe in asking when you're ready because you shall receive it when you're ready. The universe is amazing.

**What Tony Robbins taught me**
In many ways, Tony Robbins helped me set my mindset of manifestation right. I worked for Tony for a couple of years and

what I learned from him was that when you chase your dreams, make sure money is not a primary thought.

Now, the beauty of working with a leader like Tony Robbins, is that you learn by watching—his authenticity and the way he walks his talk is obvious. For example, when I was backstage and got to see what happened behind-the-scenes, I could clearly see his authenticity. The second thing I saw working with Tony was his relentless discipline: discipline in time management and strictly following the time management rules. Although it didn't always work out the discipline was there and yet the flexibility to adapt also was.

I learned from him that when you follow your dreams and your goals, the money will come anyway. So, focusing on money doesn't need to be your primary focus. There is a big difference between your drive and money management. Management is super important, what you do when the money comes in and how you use it. How do you keep money, how do you multiply it? How do you run a foundation where you can give back to society? But the drive that I saw with all the great leaders is that they have big dreams and they just go for it. Whatever it takes.

I once drove 9-10 hours for a five-minute meeting. People say, René, you're crazy! But I know why I do these things. I know that I have a mentality to do whatever it takes and I won't waste my days in excuses. That meeting ended up being a game-changer for me. My instincts knew. And that's what happens with your goals and dreams—others may look at what you're doing and think you're nuts. But it's not their dream—it's yours. It's only meant for you. That's why you receive the intuitive 'hit' and not them.

There is a huge power inside of you. By directing your mind, by visualizing your goals, by mapping your plan to success— you ignite the power and once it's aflame you have a wildfire of possibility waiting for you.

# THE IMPORTANCE OF GOAL SETTING

*"If you want to be happy, set a goal that commands your thoughts, liberates your energy and inspires your hopes."*
**Andrew Carnegie**

Reaching goals and receiving the rewards are what make us want to set the next goal. Goal setting is an action and needs to become a habit but let us make it a self-supporting habit rather than one that is detrimental to our health and wellbeing. We become what we habitually do. We are a product of all the little and big things that we habitually do. As Vincent van Gogh said, "Great things are not done by impulse, but by a series of small things brought together."[13]

American baseball player Steve Garvey said, "You have to set goals that are almost out of reach. If you set a goal that is attainable without much work or thought, you are stuck with something below your true talent and potential."

Most New Year's resolutions don't happen because people either didn't write them down, weren't specific about them, or didn't have actions to help achieve them. Research cited by the Statistic Brain Research Institute found that only 8% of people achieve their New Year's goals, which leaves a massive 92% who don't.[14]

Make goals happen by writing them down and setting actions to achieve them. People who succeed have goals, and people who have goals succeed! Psychology professor Dr. Gail Matthews from the Dominican University in California led a research study on goal setting and found that you are 42% more likely to achieve your goals if you write them down.[15] Yes, just that one small act can determine just under half of your likelihood of achieving your goal.

## WRITE AND SMILE

With that writing data in mind, when it comes to setting goals, think of something you would like to achieve in the next six months. Will you be happy if you hit this goal in the next three, six, or twelve months? Are you smiling? If the answer is yes (this is what makes you smile), then you can certainly achieve this goal. If the answer is no, go back to the drawing board and write down a goal that will make you happy if you achieve it in the timeframe you choose.

What is a goal that made you smile? Write it here:

.................................................................................................................

.................................................................................................................

.................................................................................................................

.................................................................................................................

.................................................................................................................


In what timeframe do you see yourself reaching this goal?

.................................................................................................................

.................................................................................................................

.................................................................................................................

.................................................................................................................

.................................................................................................................

If you did that simple exercise, then you are much more likely to achieve it than if you skipped over it without putting pen to paper.

Goals must be realistic and attainable. The best goals require you to stretch to achieve them, but they are not extreme. The goals are neither out of reach nor below standard performance. Goals set too high or too low become demotivating and are often ignored or procrastinated over.

When you list your goals appropriately, you develop your self-image. You see yourself as worthy of these goals and develop the traits and personality that allow you to possess them. You begin to see yourself as you wish to be.

Tip: Your goals must be things that you desire to reach, not what your partner or anyone else wants you to achieve. If the goal includes another person, they must be involved in setting the goal and choosing the reward.

*"A year from now, you will have wished you had started today."*
**Karen Lamb**

What about business goals? Yes, the same method applies. It is critical that your team or workplace set goals that involve and motivate everyone. Did you know that more than 80% of small business owners don't keep track of business goals! Astounding, right?! That's right, in the recent 4th Annual Staples National Small Business Survey, more than 80% of the 300 small business owners surveyed said that they don't keep track of their business goals and 77% have yet to achieve their vision for their company.[16]

So, let me say this: A business that sets goals and checks their progress regularly is already a step ahead of the competition.

## PURPOSE GOALS

The best day to start setting your goals is today!

Goals can be broken down into:
- **Short-term** goals that can be accomplished in days, weeks, or months and keep you focused on your medium-term goals.
- **Medium-term** goals that can usually be accomplished in months are your halfway point and keep you enthusiastic and on track to reach your long-term goals.
- **Long-term** goals will come to fruition in the future and may take months or years to be accomplished.

The length of time must be measurable, attainable, and realistic. A goal should be grounded in a timeframe, such as a target date. Commitment to deadlines helps to focus efforts on the completion of the goal on or before the due date. Goals without deadlines or schedules for completion tend to be overshadowed by the day-to-day crises that inevitably arise. With no timeframe tied to it, there is no sense of urgency.

If you want to accomplish a goal, when do you want to accomplish it by? "Someday" does not work. But if you anchor it within a timeframe, e.g., by 1 January, then you have set your unconscious mind into motion to begin working on the goal. A deadline too far into the future is too easily put off. A goal that's set with too short a timeframe may be unrealistic and discouraging. A goal is not a plan; it's more like a wish list with (hopefully) a basis in reality. Creating a plan makes that goal happen through setting short- and medium-term goals to reach the long-term goal.

Long-term goals are a description of what you want for yourself in the future, say in two to five years' time. The best way to define them is through examples, such as complete a degree, be promoted, find a life partner, double your investment account, etc.

If you are new to goal setting, it might be harder to set goals beyond three years. Start smaller, i.e., three months, six months, nine months, twelve months, eighteen months, or two years. Once you get into the flow of setting and achieving your goals, you will be able to see where you want to go and set goals further out into the future. Set a goal and shoot straight past it to even greater goals. You can recalibrate at any time. Start with just one area of your life so that you don't get overwhelmed trying to achieve it all.

Continually evaluating your goals helps you to remain conscious of your goals. Assessing and tracking your goals allows you to change course if your direction has changed, or add steps to get your goal back on track if it has fallen by the wayside.

The PURPOSE acronym is perfect for balancing purpose and goals. As I have mentioned, goals aren't as meaningful without a true sense of purpose behind them.

*"The greatest barrier to success is the fear of failure."*
**Sven Goran Eriksson**

## SET YOUR GOALS ON PURPOSE
P—Present
U—Understand
R—Relevant
P—Purposeful
O—Observe
S—Stay focused
E—Excitement

You can use these for individuals and teams.

**P:** Present your goal in a somatic and visual way through mind-mapping, goal sheets, vision boards, written versions, and visualization techniques. Look at your current goals every day.

**U:** You need to understand what it will take to achieve your goals. Understand your actions and what it will take to make these goals happen. What does the team need to do? Understanding gives you clear and measurable options to consider.

**R:** Make relevant and clear steps in the direction of your goals. Keeping the steps relevant to your outcome is the shortest road to victory. To be relevant, a goal must represent an objective toward which you are both willing and able to work. A goal can be both lofty and relevant. You are the only one who can decide just how lofty your goal should be. Your goal is relevant if you truly believe it can be accomplished. Additional ways to know if your goal is relevant are to determine whether you have accomplished anything similar in the past or to ask yourself which conditions would have to be met to accomplish the goal.

Ask yourself:
1. How can the goal be achieved?
2. What relevant actions can I take that are under my direct control?

**P:** Create a purpose statement. Check if your goals match your values and help you to lead a life worth living. Check if the purpose of your business intrinsically drives you. Ask yourself why you want to achieve this future goal.

**O:** Observe your emotions around the goal. Does it motivate and inspire you? Are the team excited and inspired by this goal?

**S:** Stay on track. Take small steps every day in the direction of your dreams. Stick your vision board in a place where you can see it each day or put it in a place where the team can view it every day. Set a weekly goal meeting to check if you're on track and staying focused.

**E:** Define how will you celebrate your achievement, even before you've attainted it. What will you or your team do when your goal is reached? Make sure this is something that really excites you or the group. Dangle the carrot of the reward and make sure you celebrate it when you get there.

*"Don't count the days, make the days count."*
**Muhammad Ali**

After you have achieved your **PURPOSE** goals, take time to **REST**:

**R**—Reflect
**E**—Evaluate
**S**—Set the Next Goal
**T**—Take Time

**R:** Take time to reflect on what you've accomplished. Ask yourself:
- How have I grown?
- What did I learn?
- What made this achievement worthwhile for me?
- What would I do better next time?

**E:** Evaluate what worked and what didn't. Ask yourself:
- Where could I improve next time?
- What should I keep doing?
- What should I change?

**S:** Set the next goal in your journey. Often, achieving one goal builds momentum for the next one. Setting your next goal is important. This doesn't mean that you need to start right away (take some time out), but it's good to get brainstorming about your next goal whilst you have momentum.

**T:** Give yourself some time out. Make sure it's not all work and no play. We need to be, not just to do. Taking time out gives you time to reflect, recover, and reevaluate. It helps to avoid burnout and falling into the trap of becoming a workaholic.

Here is a **PURPOSE** work goal example.

Your Goal: ......................................................................................................

Your Timeframe: .............................................................................................

| | |
|---|---|
| **Present** | Make a visual representation of your goal: a vision board, a mind map, a chart, or a daily screensaver with your goal listed. |
| **Understanding** | Understand what it will take to achieve your goal. |
| **Relevant** | Write a relevant step-by-step plan to help you achieve it. What will you do and when? |
| **Purposeful** | Write your purpose statement.<br>Check that your goal is congruent with your purpose statement. |
| **Observe** | Observe your emotions around this goal. Is the goal stimulating excitement and motivation for you and your team? |
| **Stay Focused** | Track and monitor your progress regularly. |
| **Excitement** | Define your workplace reward.<br>Define your personal reward. |

# REST

| | |
|---|---|
| **Reflect** | Reflect on the goal and your growth. |
| **Evaluate** | Evaluate what worked and what didn't. |
| **Set Next Goal** | Set your next goal to keep momentum. |
| **Take Time** | Take time for yourself to celebrate, rest, and reflect. |

**Exercise:** Let's begin by setting a goal for six areas of your life—a life worth leading. Categories can include:
- Career
- Family and relationships
- Health and fitness
- Personal development
- Social life
- Wealth
- You could even make a "dare to dream" section (because impossible is temporary)

Through your mind-mapping and vision board exercises, you will form a personal goal that aligns with one of your core values. Let's start by choosing a goal that excites you and that you can take action to achieve within six months. Transfer it to the PURPOSE goal planner below. Be specific with the goal. For example, you could write, "Purchase a new house on a specific land size, in a specific location with four bedrooms, three bathrooms, and two garages," instead of, "Purchase a new house." Don't worry about digging into any further detail.

Set your goal high enough for it to test you but achievable enough so that you can reward yourself for the effort and commitment. This will make you want to set more goals.

Write your goals in a positive way. If anyone is skeptical of you achieving your goals, keep them secret. Limit the dream-stealers and limit negative influences.

---

*"He who is not courageous enough to take risks will accomplish nothing in life."*
**Muhammad Ali**

---

P:_____
_____
_____

E:_____
_____
_____
_____

GOAL:

U:_____
_____
_____

S:_____
_____
_____
_____

R:_____
_____
_____

O:_____
_____
_____

P:_____
_____
_____

WHY:_____
WHAT:_____
WHO:_____
WHERE:_____
WHEN:_____

After you have completed the first goal, repeat the process with the remaining goals in each category.

Setting goals that made me lead on purpose changed my life, grew my business, and allowed me to help so many more people around the world. I know this will work for you, too. Does one life matter? Yes, it does! Do we make a bigger difference together? Yes, we do! Setting goals as a family, a team, or a corporation does make a difference. Once practiced, you will never regret the time spent setting your first goal and making it happen. The biggest decision I make each year is choosing the three goals to set or choosing to stay on target with, and letting my mind go wild on my vision board, then seeing the miracles happen throughout the year!

CHAPTER 4

# LANGUAGE FOR LEADERSHIP

## HOW WORDS IMPACT THE WAY YOU LEAD

*""One positive word has more power than a thousand hollow words. Consciously change your language for leading and you can change a moment. Change a day. Change a life."*
**Catherine Molloy**

The words you choose impact the way you lead. Leadership embodies the language you use with *yourself* each and every day. Words can be more powerful than a sword: if we can—we can; if we can't—we can't! As the great Henry Ford said, "Whether you think you can, or you think you can't—you're right."

Words (whether consciously or unconsciously) are what we use to create limitations, boundaries and opportunities. Words can stunt your personal and business growth if you don't use them properly.

*I can't*
*I'm not educated enough*
*I'm not rich enough*
*I'm too…(insert whatever you normally say after this)*
*It's not for me*
*I'm not lucky*

Boundaries get formed with our language first!

Spoken language is often different to our written language. Spoken words are direct and have the power to disempower and destroy, or empower and motivate in seconds. Whereas our written words, especially language used in business, are crafted to deliver a succinct message or retain records.

Our first language is body language, and this is what everyone sees and "reads" continuously—how we present ourselves, the flicker of emotion across our face when listening to another speak, our vocal tone and pitch, the way we stand, what we do with our hands and head movements, and whether we are temporarily distracted or not.

Language is both verbal and non-verbal.

---

*"What if the future of the world was a reflection of you?"*
**Catherine Molloy**

---

# POWER TALK

CEILs are conscious of the words they use. Changing the way you speak (both spoken and unspoken) dramatically changes your mindset and therefore the outcomes you wish to achieve.

We have all experienced incredible changes during different crises, for example COVID-19 saw many working from home yet with less connectivity with colleagues, friends and family. These new modes of operating can be unsettling, isolating and unmotivating at times. To get myself going again, I've kept telling myself, "C'mon Cath, you've got this!" A little pep talk goes a long way.

*What do you say to yourself when you need a pep talk?*

Muhammad Ali was known as the king of self-talk; he was always pumping himself up and telling himself he was "the greatest" even before he actually was. This wasn't due to an over-inflated sense of worth but because he knew what he told himself and believed—would manifest. He trained his mind through visualization and the power of self-talk. He knew his mind was eavesdropping on his self-talk.

If you want to change things in your life, be conscious of the language you use.

## CHANGE YOUR LANGUAGE

A lot of people don't particularly like change. If we remain in our comfort zone we stop growing and become sedentary. Exploring what we could change or enhance puts you back in the driver's seat of your destiny. A place we all like to be, right?

**The first step in conscious leading is changing your language and the sequence in which you do things.** For example, in a stressful situation you may default to a knee-jerk reaction of being bossy or nit-picky. Stress can often de-rail our mindful approaches and best intentions. However, if you analyze your reaction after the results, often it's too late—the damage is done. But what if you could quickly create a sequence to analyze your thoughts, reactions and outcomes *before* speaking and taking action? That would have a better outcome, right?

We all know people that don't think before they speak. Sometimes it doesn't end well, right?

A lot of people blurt things out before thinking and face the consequences once it's all too late. Conflict often begins due to knee-jerk reactions that happen in the moment. You can't take back what is already out of your mouth even if you would like to.

We must be mindful of the language we use and the silent language within our brains—what we say to ourselves and also what we say to others. Here are some common phrases that could perhaps be altered to have better outcomes.

## PROJECT POSITIVE EXPECTATIONS

| If you're going to say... | Use instead... |
| --- | --- |
| I can't | I haven't yet but I will |
| That's impossible | I know it can be done |
| I'll have to... | I would be happy to |
| I'll try | I will |

| I'd hate to... | I'd like to... |
| --- | --- |
| Another problem!? | This will create an opportunity to |
| I'm not good at... | I'm getting better at... |
| I'll have to spend more time/money | I'll invest time and money |
| Maybe you can? | When will you? |

## GIVE AND TAKE CREDIT WHEN IT'S DUE

| If you're going to say... | Use instead... |
| --- | --- |
| I got lucky | I planned well (Labor Under Correct Knowledge = L.U.C.K) |
| I don't know | This is an opportunity to learn |
| I'm so old and tired | I have lots of experience and energy |
| They did a good job | We did a good job! |

## REBOUND FROM FAILURE

| If you're going to say... | Use instead... |
| --- | --- |
| There will be bad consequences | I can see positive outcomes |
| I'm hopeless | I'm great at... |
| I failed at... | I learned so much |

## ACCEPTING RESPONSIBILITY

| If you're going to say... | Use instead... |
| --- | --- |
| It's all their fault | I take responsibility for... |
| They make me so frustrated | I feel frustrated when... |
| I don't have time | I manage my time well |

| Someone will do it | I will ensure it's done by |
| I can't alter the outcomes | I can make a difference by… |

## THE LANGUAGE FLIP

Write down 6 negative thoughts that arise for you regularly, then come up with a positive thought to replace it. For example, change, "I'm too tired to exercise today" to "If I exercise today, even just for fifteen minutes, it will fire me up for the rest of the day."

| What I usually say… | What I will say instead… |
|---|---|
| | |
| | |
| | |
| | |
| | |
| | |

## POWER WORDS

Leadership is 80% psychology, the **WHY** we do it. I always dig deep and come up with 5 whys to do something and decide before choosing to proceed. I ensure that my *whys* are in alignment with my values. The remaining 20% is mechanics—the **HOW** we do it.

Everyone says they want to grow but few want to change. And that's because change brings uncertainty. As a leader you can't control people, you can only influence people. When we use positive language for ourselves, we intentionally share this language with others and help inspire and create the change we're seeking. Power words are words we use to influence our mindset. Here is a list of power words that will motivate and create better engagement in any situation.

## THE 10 MOST HELPFUL PHRASES
1. I'd like to understand. Help me to understand.
2. How are things with you?
3. Would you like to talk about it?
4. So, what I heard you say was…
5. Let me put this another way…
6. How best may I help you?
7. What would you like to do?
8. Thank you so much!
9. I care about…
10. Use non-verbal expression to show concern: head tilts, soft eyes, gentle nods. (See *The Million Dollar Handshake* for tips about body language success.)

**Exercise:** What are the 3 most useful phrases you use?

## THE 10 LEAST HELPFUL PHRASES
1. "Don't feel that way."
2. "Why did you do that?"
3. "That's not important."
4. "I know exactly how you feel."

5. "I know what you are going to say."
6. "How come you're not as good as …?"
7. "This is what I think you should do."
8. "I'm not going to tell you I told you so."
9. "Why did you say that?"
10. Eye roll and say nothing at all

**?** **Exercise:** What are the 3 least helpful phrases you've used?

.................................................................................................

.................................................................................................

.................................................................................................

**?** What can you use instead to flip these to be helpful?

.................................................................................................

.................................................................................................

.................................................................................................

## 3 KEY LEADERSHIP SKILLS

Leaders are not leaders of others first; they are leaders of themselves. Their clarity of thought, their conviction despite the odds, and their purpose both drives and inspires excellence. Their language (both verbal and non-verbal) must reflect this.

When upskilling, we often focus on "hard" skills, technical skills such as education and training, but we also need to sharpen our "soft" skills. Soft skills are non-technical skills that relate to how you interact with colleagues, how you solve problems and how you manage your work and time. Soft skills are transferable regardless of the organization you work with, and they demonstrate your agility and flexibility. Let's explore the key soft skills required in leadership.

The 3 most important soft skills for a leader are to:
1. Communicate
2. Energize others
3. Engage others

---

*"The Conscious Leader is mindful of their emotion and emotional state to communicate, energize and engage."*
**Catherine Molloy**

---

## 1. COMMUNICATE

Communicate well by listening first. Give your undivided attention when people are talking with you. Get out of your head while others are speaking and stop yourself from formulating a reply in your mind. Refrain from nodding yes or no before they've finished speaking. Nodding can be a distraction to the person speaking with you; the person speaking may feel you are indicating for them to speed up. Yet on the plus side, it can sometimes indicate that you understand and agree with what they are saying. It's important to remember that it takes nanoseconds to form an opinion about someone or read non-verbal cues. Be still and give people the space to complete speaking, so you have all the information to respond.

Be an explorer...be curious. We really only understand the other person when we begin asking questions. Another technique is repeating back to them (in your own words) what you understand they are saying. If we don't ask questions, we accept what they are saying at face value. Asking questions gives you clarification about their how and why. For example, if someone has shared something important with you, repeat it back to them and ask if you understood it correctly. Give them the chance to correct you or say, "yes, that's right." This helps people feel heard and understood.

## PREPARATION

Effective communication involves preparation. When looking to have a conversation with a colleague, write down the key points you wish to discuss and any questions you'd like to ask. You can even write down the outcome you'd like to see from the conversation.

Next, think about the colleague's learning style: are they auditory, visual or kinesthetic? Do they prefer to talk things through or discover through reading and writing? Knowing their most dominant style helps you talk "their" language with greater clarity and increase the chances of all parties being understood. For example, I *hear* when you said..., I *see* you may need..., I *feel*..., etc.

Also note how the colleague will likely respond. Determine what is "above the line" (acceptable) versus "below the line" (unacceptable). Below the line may include no accountability or ownership, blaming others etc. If you can put it in language beforehand, it's more likely to turn out a win-win for both parties. If you react in the moment, you may get caught in emotion.

Let me repeat that in an easy three-step scenario.

Preparing your communication:
1. Write down your key points before communicating.
2. Assess who you are talking to. Are they more auditory, visual or kinesthetic?
3. Determine what is acceptable and not acceptable in your communication and response.

Planning communication like I explained above is very important for a number of reasons:
- ✓ It provides clarity and avoids going off topic.
- ✓ It avoids being swept up in the emotion when hard conversations need to be had.
- ✓ It helps each party feel included and understood (less room for miscommunication).

Let me provide an example. It was not my best leadership moment but it clearly shows things I didn't do and things I did do. It was a time I was taken by surprise and therefore not prepared (we all know this happens in life, right?).

Whilst my husband John and I had been overseas for three months, one of our team members (let's call her Jane) had been placed in the position to run the training in my absence. Upon my return we had just started a team meeting to clarify what had been happening whilst we were away. In the meeting Jane called out for "Princess" to answer a question. I was horrified. We were a close-knit team that had been working together for 5 years. We were a well-oiled machine, everyone knew their role and because of this, things ran smoothly. This is why I felt comfortable leaving Jane in charge during my absence to oversee things, although she had only joined us six months prior in a senior position, appearing to be knowledgeable and skillful in her area of expertise. It appeared that whilst I was away, instead of referring to each person by their name, Jane had given them all a nickname and no doubt, me too! This behavior went against the values of the organization, as well as my own personal values. In that moment, I did what I would normally *not* do—I reacted. I pulled Jane up right there and then in front of everyone and asked her to call each person by their name, stating that a lot of people do not like having a name made up for them and it can make them feel like they don't belong. I asked the team member that had been called "Princess" how she felt about it and she replied that she didn't like it at all. I continued with the meeting.

My reaction didn't create a win-win. In reflection, what I should have done and what I advise my clients to do, would be to call a 10-minute coffee break in the meeting right there and then and ask everyone to think about the next subject we are going to cover, and I would have then asked Jane to come into my office. I would have then let her know her behavior of calling staff invented names was totally unacceptable, it was out of alignment with the organization's vision, training and team values. It's not language for leadership when you start calling people names without their consent.

Straight after the meeting I called Jane into my office and I went through our vision, leadership skills and the care factor for each team member and asked her how she would feel about us calling her names. Jane realized it wasn't the thing to do as a leader (and by the way she was 56 years of age) but there is still more to the story.

After the meeting, another one of our staff members came up to me and advised she had been going to leave because of the name calling and the way she had been spoken to in my absence. It turns out that Jane had been using her leadership role to feel bigger and make those around her feel smaller.

Our company works with teams and this was the last thing I ever imagined our team would do!

I say, "Never walk past what you don't accept." What I mean is, if you see something and it's not acceptable, don't walk past it, talk to the person about it immediately. Otherwise, if you don't say anything, the person whose behavior was unacceptable will think that it's okay to continue with that behavior. Having said that, I would have preferred to have done this privately, as I do not believe it's a good thing to pull people up in front of teams. Our meeting had only been going for 10 minutes and my values would not allow me to continue with the meeting. I understood then and there that this created a domino effect. There is always a domino effect from every action, reaction or lack of action. If I took no action and my team didn't see me stand up for them and the values we had set in our training, I would have lost good team members that day. By taking that action, I knew that if things didn't change, I was going to lose one staff member, and that was Jane. My reaction stopped anyone else being called names during the meeting, however the action I took inevitably meant that Jane ended up leaving our team. So, fight for the people you are leading in your business, or your life.

Now, hindsight is always a good thing, and, in many instances, we may react differently if we had time to prepare…but life doesn't work that way. So, if you do have time to prepare (like a meeting with the boss, a challenging negotiation or awkward conversation) then—prepare! You are gifted the luxury of time and awareness. If you don't have time to prepare then at least determine what you consider "above" and "below" the line in terms of moral conduct, behavior and understand your domino effect.

 **Exercise:** What do you identify to be "above the line" and "below the line" with the team and company values? What is acceptable and not acceptable?

## ABOVE
---- LEVEL OF ACCEPTANCE ----
## BELOW

## THE LEVELS OF LISTENING

Have you ever noticed after speaking with someone you were missing parts of the conversation? If that's the case, you weren't really listening. There are 3 levels of listening for conscious leadership:
1. **Inner-head listening:** this is where an idea pops into your head, pay attention.
2. **Focused listening:** the person speaking has your undivided attention so you can fully understand what is being said.
3. **Global listening:** takes in the body language, tone, pitch, and energy of the speaker to get the full picture of what they are saying.

We naturally pop in and out of different listening styles, however active global listening is critical to success. The *Harvard Business Review* went a step further and analyzed the data and behavior of 3492 people taking part in a development program; the program was designed to enable managers to become more skilled coaches.[1] All participants were being assessed on their coaching skills. Throughout the process, 5% were accessed as the best listeners and then compared with the rest of the group. The researchers discovered over 20 areas in which the best listeners stood out from the active listeners. Here are the top indicators that made the excellent listeners a cut above the average (the answers may surprise you!).

- **The excellent listeners asked questions.**
  Now already this breaks a lot of myths that say, "the best listeners stay silent while the other person talks."[2] However, research tells us that asking questions that provoke thought and insight actively shows the person that you understand what they're talking about and you're interested in seeking more information or insight. A constructive or contrasting question if asked the right way evokes an interest beyond just sitting there like a good soldier and listening.

- **The excellent listeners also built a person's self-esteem.**
  The high-performance listeners made the conversation a positive experience for those involved. Excellent listeners had a special knack for making the other person feel supported and gave them a stable sense of confidence. Excellent listeners were perceived as able to create a safe environment and discuss topics with honesty and openness.

- **The excellent listeners allowed flow**
  The high-performance listeners were noted as co-operative in conversation. They allowed dialogue to flow in both directions and didn't become competitive or defensive to other people's opinions. Poor listeners however, were seen as competitive and often used the time in a conversation to think or plan their next response rather than listen. Although excellent listeners may challenge the other party or even disagree, the other person still feels that

they are trying to help rather than win an argument or get their own point across at the expense of others.

**LIVING IN THE WORLD OF COMMUNICATION**
We now live in a world of endless content and communication; this also includes technology.

Listening is one of the most important skills of the future. Listening has become a modality of choice these last few years. Think of the rise of audiobooks and podcasts. As of today's date there are over 34 million podcast episodes to listen to. Audio Publishers Association's reported that audiobook sales in the USA in 2018 was $940 million and growing by a rate of around 25% every year since 2017.[3]

Think of your Siri or Alexia or your Google Home. It's audio controlled. Voice technology is set to be a major business trend and we are now full-steam ahead into a talking, listening and audio-controlled future. What does all this equal? The power of the spoken word will never go out of fashion! It's only set to skyrocket.

According to Review 42, 72% of people who use voice search devices, claim they have become part of their daily routines.[4] And already as of 2020, 50% of all searches are voice activated with 55% of households in the US expected to own a smart speaker in 2022.

Social media, YouTube, vlogging, podcasting and sharing Insta stories is now second nature to many of us. It's communication, communication, communication. Although technology connects us, it can also disconnect us and impact our natural human skills of verbal face-to-face communication. I often tell people get the face-to-face stuff right first and then technology will follow. Those who communicate via social media but lack the "real-life" skills are only using half of their innate power.

## 2. ENERGIZE
How you energize yourself is determined by the way you communicate with yourself i.e., the 'pep' talk in your head. The same principle applies to your team.

How you show up has a domino effect on everyone you work with including what is energizing and motivating. Understanding your energy is key. Radiating positive energy, wearing a great attitude, and helping others contributes to the harmony and success of your colleagues. You inspire them to be greater. The best leaders help their colleagues get to where they need to go, creating those pathways so they can get to the next level. Whereas if you consistently show up with your body hunched over, grumbling about what happened yesterday, your attitude is a drag, it will chip away and have a detrimental effect on your team.

Your first priority is to energize yourself, then everything else flows from this positive energy. What can you do first thing in the morning and at the end of the day to keep your cup full? Start your morning with gratitude for the new adventures ahead instead of listing all the things you have to do before you've gotten out of bed. For me, at the end of every workday I go outside, take off my shoes and stand in the grass for five minutes looking at the stars. I love looking up at the night sky, it reminds me how lucky I am to live where everything sparkles (sometimes I see a shooting star), it feels incredible. Looking at the stars allows the day to slip away and I feel reenergized walking into the house to be with my family.

Another thing I do at the end of my day is what I call "DIGA"—Daily Income Generating Activity. Often, we write down a long list of to-dos and choose the ones we *feel* like doing, not what *needs* to be done. As an entrepreneur and business owner, I narrow the focus and **choose 3 tasks that will help my business grow**. These may be cold calls, warm leads, creating a post or a blog, updating a flyer, creating a new program. Preparing at the end of the day for the next day gives me the space the next morning to wake up and complete my energizing morning routine, then jump straight into the priorities I'd set the day before. My day has purpose and is in alignment with my vision, and not at the ebb and flow of tasks that maintain but don't grow my business.

**Exercise:** What 3 things can you do in the morning and/or evening to feel energized?

.................................................................................................................

.................................................................................................................

.................................................................................................................

Energy is a form of communication. Enhance your positive vibes and radiate them out to all.

## 3. ENGAGE

Think of a great leader you've worked with (either current or past), what did you love about that time? Was it their ability to communicate well with you? Did they raise the energy of the room when they walked into the business? Did they engage you in what was happening? Were they approachable?

A great leader will make decisions that need to be made. They may not always be right, but they will continually improve.

A great leader will ask their team for help when they need it. They will be able to engage their team to help them get to that next level as well. While a leader is solution-focused, they encourage their team to become solution-focused also.

Let's say the government changes the regulations and this affects a project you're working on. You look at it as a great opportunity, you know that pivoting will allow growth for the company, and you decide on the new direction without the team's input and then ask the team to implement it. Without team input and collaboration, it may leave them feeling "here we go again, he/she thinks they know everything." Whereas if you initially throw back to them and say, "see if you can come up with a couple of ideas and come back to me, then we'll sit down and work out the best solution." This approach will leave the team feeling empowered to seek and engage alternate solutions for discussion. If the end result is something else, then a leader would ensure everyone is in agreement and happy to implement. How you engage others is very important. What language are you using? Inclusive "we" language or polarizing "me" language?

Science shows that using "we" language rather than "me" language helps people feel included and identified within the tribe.[5] Using language that promotes "we" and "us" is a small thing to do with massive positive outcomes. "Our" team is more inclusive than "my team."

> Here are some inclusive examples:
> *We did great today on this project!*
> *Our new clients are so happy with us.*
> *What decision do you think we should make?*
> *What is best for our team?*
> *How can we improve as a team?*

## EXCEPTIONS TO EVERY RULE

Recently Daniel McGinn interviewed Jerry Seinfeld on the HBR IdeaCast, and Jerry said, "The show was successful because I micromanaged it—every word, every line, every take, every edit, every casting."[6] Usually, micromanagement is hard to sustain for long periods of time, stifles creativity and efficiency, and reduces job satisfaction. However, there are exceptions—like Jerry Seinfeld! Every project will have someone managing it, even if you set a goal you need to manage it to make it happen. So, managing and micromanaging isn't really the problem, it's the way you go about it, it's the *language* you use with the people you are working with and the attitude you bring to each project.

One of my strengths is input—I love getting information, understanding how it all works. I was "that" kid, always following my dad around and asking, "but how?" and "but why?" If 1 + 1 doesn't equal 2 in my head, then I'd have to go back to the drawing board and figure out why.

You can imagine my children (having a mother as a body language expert) must have felt like I was in the secret service because I always knew when something wasn't right. As a leader, I'm very strategic around input and whilst checking in with my team I had to be careful so as not to be perceived as micromanaging them. This is why it's important for you and your team to understand everyone's strengths. Me asking questions was because I was curious to learn, not because I was checking up on others.

If you understand your strengths and how they can be perceived, you can change your language so it doesn't come across negatively. There is a reason why conscious leadership is said to be the most important or crucial aspect in business and the entrepreneurial world today, because it takes effort and awareness in the practice of being fully aware of oneself and fully present in the moment. And language and communicating is a huge aspect of this.

## THE LANGUAGE OF EMOTIONAL INTELLIGENCE

As I mentioned earlier, we all respond to situations differently. When we are stressed or caught unawares, sometimes our behavior defaults into a destructive one rather than a constructive one.

**Constructive behaviors** trigger positive emotions, builds upon experience and provides positive steps for future experiences.

**Destructive behaviors** trigger negative emotions and provoke defensiveness. To release negative behaviors you need to replace them consciously with positive constructive behaviors. You don't necessarily eliminate them; you merely don't give them room to thrive. Replace them purposefully with positive constructive behaviors.

Examples of destructive and constructive behavior for leadership:

| Destructive | Constructive |
|---|---|
| Judging others | Using active listening |
| Being aggressive and sarcastic | Being honest and open |
| Dismissing opinions of others | Discussing issues and situations |
| Unnecessarily questioning opinions | Being inclusive |
|  | Being proactive |
| Using personal attacks | Focusing on conversations |

**Exercise:** Take a moment to clear your mind, then answer the following honestly:
- Do you **react** or **respond** when under pressure?
- How do people perceive you when under pressure?
- Are you always behind catching up with work or are you purposely moving forward on your most strategic work?

Take a look at your answers. You can consciously start to see how you are likely to behave and respond in any situation. Is there anything you'd like to change?

## THE 5 CONSCIOUS LEADERSHIP PRACTICES FOR LANGUAGE, MINDSET & BEHAVIOR

I believe there are 5 practices to adopt in order to be a Conscious Leader. These practices create the space to assist you in leading, to be the best version of yourself. They include:

1. Be mindful, not mind-full
2. Make time for self-reflection
3. Practice having routines
4. Use "WE" rather than "ME"
5. Ego—leave it behind

Let's dive into each of these conscious leadership practices.

## BE MINDFUL, NOT MIND-FULL

When our mind is full, when it's continuously thinking of what you've still got to get through: work, deadlines, managing people, what's going on outside work hours, your personal life—it's easy to become overwhelmed.

However when you are mindful, you are aware of your body, your mind, your feelings in the present moment, and what you need to change to create a feeling of calm. You're then being mindful of who is speaking, being mindful of your surroundings, being mindful of the planet, being mindful of the universe, being mindful of your language.

The practice of analyzing before reacting and speaking is what conscious leadership (mindful leadership) is all about.

*"Be a thoughtful leader,
not just a thought leader."*
**Catherine Molloy**

**Exercise:** List some ways you can go from being mind-full to mindful.

## SELF-REFLECTION

The *Cambridge Dictionary* defines self reflection as: the activity of thinking about your own feelings and behavior, and the reasons that may lie behind them.

At the end of each day, take five minutes to reflect on the events of the day and assess yourself as a leader. What are your thoughts? How do you react to these emotions? How is your body reacting? What can you do or could have done to make the situation better?

Self-reflection allows us to step out of our head and assess what is required to move forward, and helps us reflect whether our own needs are being met.

You may reflect on simple behaviors like:

*Am I eating a balanced diet?*
*Am I eating enough?*
*Am I getting the exercise I need?*
*Am I getting enough sleep?*
*Are my stress levels under control?*

You may need to reflect on situations that occurred or past behaviors. You may have a situation where you weren't as alert as you usually are due to fatigue, and as a result you may have reacted rather than listened, assessed and actioned. Self-reflection helps us take stock of the situation and *reflect to perfect*.

**Exercise**: Schedule 5-10 mins at the end of your workday to self-reflect on these questions and the language you use. Ask yourself:
- What went well today and why? How did that make me feel?
- Were there any situations that could have gone differently today? What could I improve?
- Did I actively listen to what was being raised?
- Did I react, or gather all the information before responding?
- Is there anything that could have been done better?

## PRACTICE HAVING ROUTINES

Daily practices or repetitive routines assist with cultivating awareness and consciousness. Having routines creates habits...and habits are the driving force for success. Simple yet effective practices can include: 5-minute morning and/or evening meditations, deep breathing exercises to calm the mind and body, enjoy a quick lunch time walk. And at the end of the workday, set 3 important tasks for the following day, and time for reflection at the end of every workday.

**Exercise:** What micro-habits can you create to help you relax, focus and succeed?

.................................................................................................

.................................................................................................

.................................................................................................

.................................................................................................

.................................................................................................

## USE THE LANGUAGE OF "WE" RATHER THAN "ME"

Being a conscious leader requires great amounts of determination, patience and understanding. A leader's role is about creating and cultivating a workplace where trust and care of the whole (not just the individual or self) is of paramount importance. Understanding people before judging and reacting is a key factor in regard to this. Including others and coming from a place of "us" is a great foundation.

## THE DIFFERENCE BETWEEN

| BOSS | LEADER |
|---|---|
| Drives employees | Guides employees |
| Ensures authority | Depends on teamwork |
| Ignites fear | Ignites enthusiasm |
| Uses the word "I" | Uses the word "We" |
| Places blame on others | Takes responsibility |
| Knows how it's done | Teaches how it's done |
| Uses people | Grows people |
| Takes credit | Gives credit |
| Commands | Asks |
| Says "Do it" | Says "Let's do it" |

Did you know that over 60 percent of consumers say their perception of a CEO affects their opinion of the company as a whole?[7]

## EGO—LEAVE IT BEHIND

Egos are the most difficult to let go of because we want to be right and not fail. What would happen if you let go of being right? What we think is right is not always correct. It's not always what you believe that makes you a better person—it's only your point of view. It's the way you behave that makes you a leader. When you completely understand and accept this, it will allow for a more empowered and motivated organisation. You are there to support and guide people to reach their goals and potential, your ego needs to take a back seat.

Being mindful and understanding of behaviors and nonverbal communication allowed me to embrace and engage people in a whole new way and build a global business. Practicing these conscious leadership principles will get you through every crisis, just as I did when John's health took a turn for the worse during the GFC. As many people in the world today are experiencing and living through a crisis, leading ourselves well makes all the difference. It's about being aware of your actions and making positive conscious decisions today because your decisions today create your tomorrow. The pattern of our self-talk language is what we're saying to ourselves when we make a decision. When we make an ego-based decision, we cut off and kill all other possibilities.

 **Exercise:** Look at the conscious leadership practices (Be mindful, not mind-full. Make time for self-reflection. Practice having routines. Use "WE" rather than "ME". Ego—leave it behind) and circle which one you're doing really well and which one you would like to improve.

**The practice I'm doing well is** _____

**The practice I need to improve is** _____

The reason you are doing this is to anchor yourself in what you do well so you keep doing it, and identify a practice you would like to utilize more to become a more conscious leader. If you find yourself wanting to circle more than one area, that's okay, but make sure you focus on one at a time until it becomes a habit.

## GROWING YOUR MIND-LANGUAGE

*"If you change the way you look at things, the things you look at change."*
**Wayne Dyer**

What is it you are saying to yourself? Catch every thought that crosses your mind for three days and you'll have an insight into your self-talk. Do you criticize yourself, or do you acccept yourself and strive for greater?

Through self-reflection, you learn to process your thoughts and feelings, and understand why you feel the way you do. Understanding and being in control of your thoughts and feelings is one of first steps to changing your behavior for the better (and achieving your goals).

To reinforce your new mindset, keep a collection of inspirational quotes and review them daily.

Here are some examples of growth mindset thoughts:
- I am making a difference
- I am grateful for today
- I can…
- I am taking action
- I'm prepared
- I'm creating positive results
- I'm happy
- I consciously communicate with others
- I am continually learning
- I am responsible for my own actions
- I am choosing positive language to lead with

**Exercise:** List 6 new growth mindset thoughts you can start using.

It is human to have negative thoughts and it's important to let them come, acknowledge them and then let them go. Don't dwell on anything for too long, replace the thought with something positive.

*"Once you change your philosophy, you change your thought pattern. Once you change your thought pattern, you change your attitude. Once you change your attitude, it changes your behavior pattern and then you go on into some action."*
*Malcolm X*

## WALKING YOUR TALK
### *AN INTERVIEW WITH ELAINE JOBSON (C.E.O JETTS FITNESS)*

Few CEOs have climbed up the business ranks through sheer tenacity and street smarts like Elaine Jobson; recognized globally for her success working at senior executive levels in the fitness industry for the world's top entrepreneurs such as Mike Balfour and Richard Branson.

I was thrilled that Elaine was happy to share her leadership experiences from her time in business for this book. And more specifically, share with me what she learnt from past leaders that she incorporates into her own leadership style today, and even those surprising traits she learned from the bad ones.

**Q. Who has been a great leader that you've worked with?**
I would say you get different things from different people. A bad leader I had actually taught me some good things. But one of the best leaders I worked for was Terry Kew who was Global Sales Director for Fitness First at the time. He was actually living in Australia and I was working as the National Sales Manager in the UK.

His reputation preceded him; I kept hearing about this person who created these rock star, superstar people [salespeople?], these skilled, amazing performers and really good leaders.

I've always had this thing of seeking out leaders to work for, seeking out brands to work for. So I actually made it a bit of a mission to work for him. I had the opportunity to move up into a European Sales Director role for the company, and as the Global Sales Director, Terry became my boss. I was quite young at the time and wanted to understand what he did to make people so good.

He had this great discipline of going through expectations when we first met. He'd say here's all the things I expect of you and then he'd ask what expectations I had for him. It's actually a tangible skill that I've consistently done with every team member that reports to me; I got that from him.

When I first met him, he said one of his expectations was for me to take 10% of my salary and invest it back into myself. I was 26 or so and living the life in London so I wasn't too keen on this idea. But he persisted, telling me you're going to be better because of it, you only get paid for what you know and what you're worth.

So I did as he said, very begrudgingly for the first year I admit. After a few years I sat back and realized what I could do. This saving paid for my Tony Robbins courses. I did Zig Ziglar, Jim Collins, Stephen Covey, learning from all these amazing leaders, trainers and facilitators. I did Harvard Business study and business leadership courses at Cranfield University.

There's no way on earth I would have been able to spend $20,000 on a business course at that age if it wasn't for him "making" me do it. Suddenly this world of opportunity opened up, I could go and almost learn anything. I actually have to give credit to him for where I am today and where I got to quite quickly in terms of age.

He did want me to be careful who taught me. I had to be able to justify who it was, to really do my research and make sure that it's quality. Someone with proven business acumen to back up what they're teaching you: someone who has walked the talk.

I know there are other more charismatic or well-known leaders that I've worked with, but Terry has been the most practically impactful. His teachings made a significant shift in my capabilities to do the job that I do today.

That's probably why I say less inspiration, more perspiration.

**Q. Have you worked with someone with an ineffective leadership style?**
This is so easy for me. It was an early boss. He was a real entrepreneur, quite young, only a few years older than me at the time but he made me call him Mr Campbell. He was this angry Scottish guy, angry at the world and ferociously wanted to get on and wanted to be a millionaire. He had a lot of challenges in his life, so he was very motivated, but he had no leadership training himself and had a very narrow view on what leadership was.

He had two gyms in Glasgow and Edinburgh and wanted to expand into England with a gym in Leeds. It was a massive sales driven organization. To be honest, he taught me to sell and I became quite a competent salesperson through his methods, and I became his kind of national sales and marketing manager.

He used to do these things in the office where he would literally scream at people, swear at people at the top of his voice, throw things at people: it was horrific. He would never get away with any of that nowadays obviously. He was quite abusive on a whole other level.

He used to play favorites, giving you praise and gifts in front of everyone if you performed well. If you weren't going so well, he would do the opposite and belittle you in front of everyone; that was his culture. He would drive us really hard and I guess that's something he instilled in me quite early, to work really hard. If you weren't doing 18 hours a day, you were nobody.

People would start with him in the business and he would put them through the wringer, be really abusive to them. Then when he felt that you'd coped with enough abuse and managed to survive, he started to kind of like you and he'd give you a mug that said *I can cope* on it.

His leadership style of abuse probably burnt out a lot of talented people because they couldn't tolerate the environment he created. He paid well and was good at moving the money around to get results and we went from 3 gyms to 30 within a short period of time. But as you're growing a company you rely on the goodwill and loyalty of your people but when he got to a certain size, he couldn't be hands on anymore with every single person. He wanted complete control.

He was so crippling as a leader; he stifled creative thinking, collaboration, teamwork. It became a lot of ambitious, quite ruthless individuals in the end. It wasn't sustainable. He went into liquidation almost as fast as he grew.

I knew I had to get out because it wasn't going to end well. I had to get physically away from him because he was so controlling. I moved to London, but he tracked me down to see if I would come back to work for him.

I've often thought back and wondered why I stayed with him so long. I didn't want to be a quitter; I wanted to show that I could stand up to it, that I could survive. I was a bit of a buffer for the team. I am an incredibly resilient person; I know I am. I was probably one of the few people he did invest in, he could see that I was quite career-oriented and enabled me to satisfy a lot of my own personal goals. Maybe I owe my resilience to him.

**Q. Was there a time you felt you could have led better?**
Probably not too long after this bad leadership experience, I obviously hadn't honed all my leadership skills at this point. I was running a sales team, and sales in the fitness industry was quite aggressive back then.

I had a culture of working hard because that's what I'd come from. I did invest and train the team a lot better, but I did work them hard. So January and February are always the biggest sales months and we had had an absolute phenomenal, record-breaking New Year period.

In the first week of March, I went into my sales office and saw an envelope on my desk. Inside were two tickets to the Caribbean! I wasn't a holiday taker, but this was amazing for me to see these two tickets to go on holiday.

I knocked on my boss's office with the envelope in my hand. He was on the phone but abruptly pointed for me to sit down and I thought it was weird that he looked a bit pissed off. He finished his conversation and turned to me and said, "Don't you ever do that again!" I didn't know what he was talking about. "Have you seen your team? Have you any idea?"

I still thought he was referring to the massive 8 weeks of selling, doing the best we'd ever done and so I tried to thank him for the tickets. But then he became clear, "You need to learn such a lesson. It's one thing to put yourself through that but it's quite another to put the whole fricking team through that. They are an absolute mess. Tell me when was the last time you took a day off?" I told him it was at Christmas.

"You haven't taken a day off for 8 weeks and neither has your team! When was the last time you had a workout? When was the last time you actually invested back into yourself? You're knackered and you're of no use to me whatsoever. Those tickets are to force you to take time off and leave your team the hell alone. Go and sit on a Caribbean island and figure out how you're going to do things better."

He helped me understand about burning out and how important it is to be healthy and rested. That my way of running the team had not been sustainable. I had a lovely bouquet of flowers in the hotel room when I arrived in the Caribbean. I opened the nice-looking card and inside my boss had written; *Next time, I'll fire you.*

So you've got to look after yourself before you look after others. It had all been about chasing down the result and not looking after the team. That was my lesson on being a bad leader and driving my team like dogs.

I wasn't married or had any kids then, so I could work long hours. It was quite selfish actually. I found the humility and apologized to the team. My nickname used to be "Five More," because I would always say, "Yeah, but can you get me five more?" Now I know you can push your team to get 5% more results but there's going to be an exponential price that you'll pay for that. It was learning to do five less and actually feel good about it.

Or at least, to not have anxiety attacks if we're not pushing fifth gear all the time.

**Q. When have you led yourself well?**
A favorite time for me was definitely working in South Africa. It has an amazing back story in that Nelson Mandela actually phoned Richard Branson up asking if he'd consider buying a huge gym franchise whose owners had all just been arrested for something and the business was going into liquidation, leaving more than 5000 employees out of work overnight.

Richard agreed to buy it and so I was one of the executive team whose mandate was to turn it into a Virgin company, to create a culture that supported the values of what Virgin is all about. We were met with a really poor situation. The gangster-types that had owned the business had ingrained a culture of absolute fear into the company, fear of everything.

So at first, I tried all these different ways of measuring employee engagement: free breakfasts, add a foosball table for the staff, have a day off on your birthday. It didn't seem to matter, nothing made a difference, nothing was sticking.

So I did what I always do when I don't understand what's going on, I went into the gym to work with the teams and try and see for myself. I think coming from the ground up has helped; I haven't sat in universities and then gone in at executive level.

So I worked alongside the club manager for a while, just to observe and understand. While I was in the gym, one of the maintenance team (these were massive gyms with 40 employees in one gym) came up to us with a gash in his arm. The employee had had a mishap with a screwdriver and the wound obviously needed stitches.

The manager and I told him to go and get himself stitched up at the hospital and look after himself. A few days later, I was back with the club manager and I asked how that employee was. To which the manager replied they hadn't seen him since his he left.

Most of our team lived in townships often with no phones so they could be hard to track down. We jumped in the car and asked around if anyone had seen him near his home. No one had so we backtracked to the hospital.

We actually found him still in the hospital 56 hours after we'd last seen him. He'd been waiting so long in the waiting room that septicaemia had set into the wound. He had gone into septic shock and was sent into intensive care. He ended up having his arm amputated from the elbow down.

I was devastated by this; I couldn't believe what had happened. I went back to the team, got the whole team together and said I just need to understand what happened here.

The team said they couldn't really get seen when they go to hospital because they didn't have medical aid. In South Africa, most companies would pay for this for their people and is effectively a basic grade of medical insurance.

It is optional though and the previous gangster owners had never wanted to spend the money to put this into place. I guess being a British company, we never really understood what it was. So I did my research and understood that medical aid was a really important part of an employee's package. It was essentially the difference between them being able to walk into a doctor's and be seen or walk into a doctor's and be put to the back of the queue, literally put behind every other person that had a medical aid card.

I went and spoke to the board and even though it wasn't cheap to implement, the board agreed. There was this wave of happiness that went across the team, just about feeling comfortable and certain about their health and their family's health. It shouldn't take a guy losing half his arm to understand the importance of putting this in. We should have known this right from the beginning.

This was a revolution. From being effectively hated by people in the company, to being loved overnight. They didn't want a free breakfast or a foosball table; they just wanted to feel safe. This propelled us forward to eventually becoming one of the best places to work, winning the Deloitte Award for Best Place to Work in South Africa.

That situation was when I was most proud of my leadership, to be small enough to go down to the lowest level, but also to be able to get it up to a board to make a decision that would impact 5-10,000 people.

**Q. What top qualities make up good leadership?**
Walking the talk. I'm very conscious of not being led by people that haven't done what they're talking about. Integrity would be wrapped up in there too.

Also, taking responsibility. I loved a keynote story I heard by Rudy Guiliani, past mayor of New York. When he first took the role, he called all the different departments into a meeting and asked them to tell him what was wrong with New York. The councillors, the police chief and the others started bickering and blaming each other. Giuliani just came and wrote *I'm responsible* so they all could see. He told them to stop blaming each other and blame him.

Leadership is about taking responsibility, warts and all. I think compassion and humility comes through that. Even if it may not be your fault, as a leader, you take that on as well.

In line with compassion, is being kind and I know that sounds easy. But it's about being kind in the moments when it's not traditional. People will come and go from companies, not everybody is suited. I remember bringing in a guy who'd worked for me before and I promoted him into a higher role, he didn't go very well. I'd made an error in recruiting him but when I let him go, I was as kind as possible.

That sort of thing should never come as a surprise. You should be able to point to all the opportunities to provide feedback and hold the mirror up.

I let him go as kindly as I could. It took ten years, but he eventually called me up again and said, "I just want to say, what you did to me ten years ago was the kindest thing you could ever do. I was shit at that role and you made me leave." He'd gone on to own his own training company and had amazing success. So kindness is really important even in moments that you know seem unkind.

Elaine Jobson is a leader who inspires action. Acknowledging how much the practical language of her past leaders has enabled her success today, she has little time for rhetoric or the blame game and knows how detrimental it is to creating a healthy team and healthy culture. Elaine's story shows the importance of spending time at the frontline, walking the talk and learning how to listen to the heart of the story.

My first meeting with Elaine was literally up against a wall. We were both in dresses looking a little uncomfortable (I know I'd rather be in a pair of pants or leggings). We were in a room with a thousand people looking fabulous. We said "Hi" had a few laughs, some champagne and then found out our tables were at the back of the room next to each other near the dancefloor. After Elaine won outstanding businesswoman of the year, we danced the night away. Elaine was humble, quiet, reserved, confident and great fun to be around. What I know is first impressions do matter and you never really know who you are connecting with until you take the time to find out their story.

## SELF-REFLECTION ON WALKING YOUR TALK

Elaine's experiences offer a whole range of wisdom. One is the importance of self-reflection and feedback. Self-reflection is a chance to give ourselves feedback, which is important in developing consciousness of self. Feedback gives you information about what you do well and where you could improve. It allows you to:
- Reflect on your thoughts and words
- Understand any strengths and weaknesses
- Clarify any inconsistencies in your actions
- Make any changes or improvements to be able to better achieve the outcomes you would like.

Did you know that leaders spend 75 to 80 percent of their working hours communicating.[8] That's a huge amount of time! Wouldn't it be worth investing in doing it well?

Assistant professor of management at The University of Texas at San Antonio (UTSA), Jonathan R. Clark says that the language of leaders has a profound impact on the performance of their team. Clark's report and research published in *Organizational Dynamics*, reveals that how a company presents its vision and values is deeply rooted in its overall success.[9] Simply a change in titles and language can go a long way. For example, his study mentioned a health care clinic in Cleveland USA that had the CEO of that company communicate a new vision to the staff—using emotive language and ensuring that every employee was referred to as a "care giver"—this went for everyone—from surgeons, to nurses and janitors. This language helped form a deep connection to their vision and values. Clark said, "language that leaders use is absolutely critical." He went on to highlight that "A leader provides focus for people and points them toward a specific set of values that guide action within the organization."

*"When you change your language, you change your life."*
**Catherine Molloy**

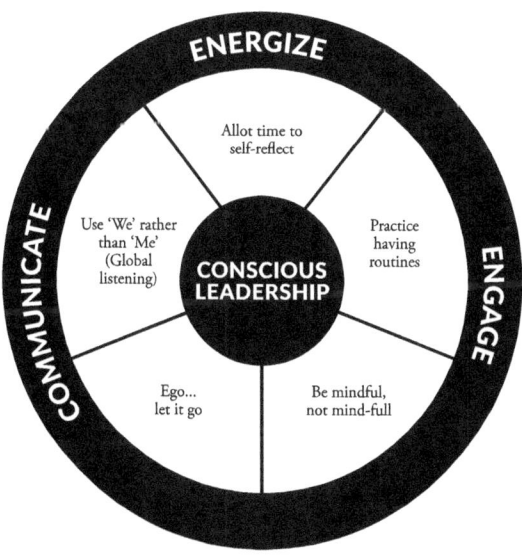

CHAPTER 5

# LEADING OTHERS

## INSPIRING AND MOTIVATING TEAMS THROUGH CRISES AND BEYOND

*"Leadership is not just a position,
it is a conscious decision."*
**Catherine Molloy**

We tend to think that leaders have it all figured out—they have the answers to everything. I'm here to let you know this is a myth. Leaders are just further along their journey of self-discovery than others. They know the values that are most important to them and how these values align with the organization. They understand their own strengths and weaknesses, how to best work with them, and how they are perceived by others. They have developed their soft skills and know the power of words, and regularly use the five conscious leadership practices. The next step on their journey is inspiring individuals and teams to be the best they can be.

Let's point out another myth: climbing the ranks is the way to develop leadership. In fact, the leader is not necessarily the one people want to follow. As Simon Sinek so eloquently points out, "Leading is not the same as being the leader. Being the leader means you hold the highest rank, either by earning it, good fortune or navigating internal politics. Leading however, means that others willingly follow you—not because they have to, not because they are paid to, but because they want to."

Leaders try to gain influence in a number of ways. Here are three ways that I have seen used very commonly within leadership ranks. They all work to a degree, but some have bigger consequences than others.

## USING THE LANGUAGE OF FEAR

Some people in levels of influence attempt to use the language of fear and panic; for example, they might use an employee's job security as leverage. When fear is used, people often follow with little questioning. Hitler is a great example of a leader who used fear as propaganda, preaching that he would rescue the country from the grip of depression. Another example is the media frenzy around COVID-19, which induced panic buying of toilet paper, pasta, rice, and sanitizer. In my personal opinion, using fear isn't a good foundation for leadership. It is a manipulative tool to get people to do what you want and is not recommended.

## MOTIVATING BY INCENTIVES

Some leaders use incentives and strategically dangle rewards. But incentives can backfire—people may feel they're being pitted against someone else, or the task or reward may not be in alignment with their values. Instead, have the whole team meet, brainstorm, and work together for the outcome. If you do use incentives, find out what truly motivates people. Often, people would rather have time in lieu or flexible work hours than money.

## FEIGNING CERTAINTY

The Cambridge Dictionary defines certainty as "the state of being completely confident or having no doubt about something." While complete confidence can be reassuring, it is important to be truthful to inspire others to the next level. People want the truth so that they can make decisions. When in positions of management or leadership, be truthful about where the business is going. Let the team know whether there are any bumps and how these could be handled, and once they've absorbed the information, ask them what they want to do. It's just as important to communicate what is going well as it is to point out what is not.

In the movie *A Few Good Men*, Jack Nicholson's character delivers the famous line: "You can't handle the truth!" The phrase suggests that leaders need to hold things back to protect others. But is that the case?

I believe that once we start making judgments about what people can or can't handle, we are not being open or truthful to ourselves or others. Everyone has the right to know the truth and make decisions accordingly. A business may have an open door policy, but if managers are not honest and open with the team, the team will not be honest or open with them. It is not only an open door that is required but an open mind and an open heart.

## WHAT TYPE OF LEADER IS NEEDED IN A CRISIS?

No leader is perfect. A conscious leader does the best they can with the skills they have and understands that they are on a path of continual learning. Knowing who the stakeholders and customers are and setting leadership goals is of the utmost importance. While the team usually focuses on the customer or client, a leader is also responsible to each and every team member. Leaders should treat their team in exactly the same way they treat six- or seven-figure customers.

A Gallup® poll asked more than 10,000 followers what they looked for in leaders during the COVID-19 crisis. Their answers reflect what people need from their leaders in any time of severe uncertainty: **trust, compassion, stability, and hope.**[1]

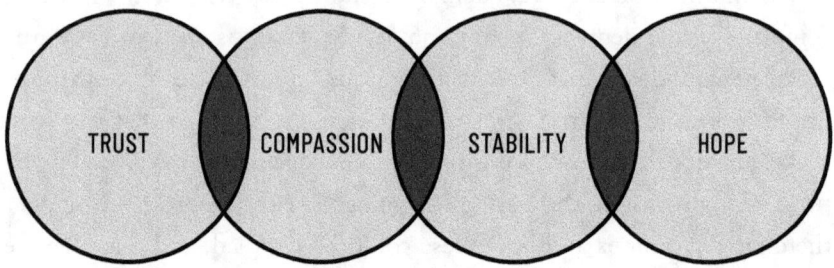

When everything is unsteady and uncertain, people look for stability and certainty. Poise and strength are required when heads are spinning and hearts are thumping with fear and worry.

The question is: do you have what it takes?

Good leaders:
- Help others to create, not to conform
- Guide, persuade, and reassure those with whom they travel
- Clarify rather than confuse
- Support and confirm rather than replace
- Listen fairly, without unnecessary judgment
- Pay attention and motivate others
- Draw out rather than push away
- Unify rather than conquer
- Encourage rather than discourage
- Free rather than limit
- Grant independence rather than maintain dependence
- Lead by example and walk the talk

Workplace effectiveness means making the most of the time that you have at work. It is important for teams to prioritize their work tasks, set daily and weekly goals, and then check in and manage the process to ensure that the job is being done to the organization's standards.

There are two common leadership approaches:
- Hands-on leaders manage all meetings, check in with team members, and are communicative, energizing and engaging without micromanaging.
- Some leaders prefer to set up teams and provide them with information for the project. Once the team has come together and completed their SWOT analysis, the leader will move on to another project, providing input or checking in only when required. This type of leader must ensure that others on the team have the skills to communicate, energize, and engage for the project's success.

There is no right or wrong choice; the right approach often depends on the project. A leader may even switch back and forth between these approaches across multiple projects, depending on each team's skill set.

I remember being in an organization in which senior management sat upstairs and the administration team sat downstairs with an open floor plan. There were two individuals who would spend a lot of time chatting while others sat nearby trying to get their work done. The two would have a great old yak regularly, and the sound traveled upstairs. Their attention to detail began to slip, they started making simple mistakes, and they were distracting and annoying the people around them. When colleagues asked them for assistance, they replied they had too much work. One of the two ended up being retrenched, and shortly after that, the other left because they were no longer happy in their job. If you were the leader, how would you have handled this situation?

In this example, a conscious leader would call a single meeting with both individuals and another leader. They would begin with a positive ("It's great you two connect") but then explain how sound travels throughout the office and their conversation has become distracting. They would point out the relevant mistakes that occurred. The goal of such a meeting is to clarify the situation and ask the people involved to work out how to make improvements. They may suggest rearranging the office seating or another plan—the point is to let them come up with something that would work.

Another thing to note is that if a team member comes to you with complaints about another team member and you haven't seen or experienced the issue yourself, you need to collect information before taking action. If you are unable to put yourself in a position to observe the behavior, then you could interview everybody and ask how the project is coming along and whether they have any concerns. In this way, you will learn if this situation is arising with other colleagues or if it is just one person's opinion. Never blame others.

**Be a thoughtful leader, not just a thought leader.**

If you have jumped to the wrong conclusion or reacted with emotion as opposed to leading consciously, be humble, be honest, and apologize. Ask the person(s) you're speaking with how they are feeling and how they have been affected. Ask for forgiveness, and make sure the other party feels that the issue has been resolved. Without these little conversations, trust is easily broken. Be approachable. Have an open door policy so people can connect with you. Have empathy. Allow your staff to make mistakes, and help them be solution-focused. Most importantly, learn from your team—they'll be the first ones to show you what's not working.

## DIFFICULT OR DIFFERENT?

There are certain types of people who may tend to be seen as difficult to work with in the eyes of others. They usually fall into the following categories:

- The stubborn one—a person who is set in their ways and rarely strays outside the box
- The quiet one—a person who keeps their opinions to themselves
- The jester—a person who always likes to joke around
- The chatterbox—a person who likes to find out what's going on and may inadvertently share information

- The know-it-all—a person who has all the answers, which can be off-putting for others
- The whiner—a person who sees the cup as half full

I'm sure you've come across all of these characters in your career and on your teams. You may yourself be one of them. The best way to help different types of people communicate and work together well is to understand each person's learning style and the strengths they contribute to the team.

## EMOTIONAL INTELLIGENCE WITHIN A TEAM

To be an effective team leader, you need to be able to harness the emotional and practical strengths of individual team members. To do this, you should identify a worker's strengths and allocate jobs or tasks based on those strengths. This can also be done in relation to the team as a whole.

This approach will maximize the team's efficiency, productivity, and performance outcomes and improve morale for individual workers. The strengths to look out for include emotional intelligence, good work ethic, consistency, determination, motivation, reliability, flexibility, practical skills, group focus, efficiency, good communication skills, etc.

There are several actions you can take to maximize a group's strengths:
- Select projects with tasks that maximize the strengths of individual work group members and those of the work group as a whole.
- Identify the emotional strengths of work group members, and delegate tasks based on these strengths.
- Balance a work group's tasks so that the strengths of different individuals contribute to the efficiency of the group as a whole.
- Encourage cooperation and collaboration between work group members.
- Monitor progress but encourage autonomy so that members apply their skills.
- Encourage work group members to report any mistakes and use these as learning experiences.

- Give constructive feedback to reinforce the group's strengths and help them successfully achieve the required outcomes.
- Recognize and reward outstanding achievements.
- Celebrate work group outcomes.
- Celebrate wins both big and small.
- Encourage feedback from work group members on their contribution, and encourage any ideas for improvement.
- Strengthen the emotional wellbeing of work groups by regularly giving feedback about how their cohesion contributes to their outcomes.

Sometimes working well within a team is just a matter of understanding each person's particular style. For example, when our training business begins working with a company, the first people we work with are the CEO and the leadership team. We look at their talents and strengths and where they may be perceived differently by others. Suppose the CEO is a forward thinking, big-picture, quick-starter type who can communicate the vision and change track when needed. These are all assets, but when this person moves too quickly, they may leave others behind. Some people may not be visual or may need time to digest the vision—they can feel like they're not being listened to or given enough detail. In this situation, we would work with the CEO on listening techniques, such as global listening (using the environment or body language), asking more questions to gather information before replying, and role play.

With daily practice, these skills become habit. When we follow up with teams after this type of training, it is always incredible to see the positive change in dynamics and culture. It wasn't that they didn't work well together before the training; it's just that they collaborate even better when they know, like, and trust each other and understand their individual styles. In other words, when a leader becomes more conscious and emotionally intelligent, they can create positive outcomes across the entire team.

## DECISION-MAKING

Developing good relationships also depends on making good decisions. Decision-making in the workplace is often driven by emotions. Therefore, developing emotional intelligence can greatly improve your decision making. Empathy and social awareness will help you make decisions that respect the thoughts and feelings of others.

Once you have developed your ability to read the emotional cues of your work group members and have become more familiar with each individual, you can anticipate their likely emotional responses to your decisions. As an example, some workers might focus on the options that were not chosen. In this situation, use your emotional intelligence to immediately redirect their focus towards the positive benefits of the decision.

The initial emotional responses of your work group members to your decisions are likely to reflect their reflexive feelings. These responses are not necessarily linked to the decision you have made but to their individual triggers, emotions, and past experiences. Here are some tips to help you bear in mind the emotions of others when making decisions:

- Practice focused, active listening.
- Read nonverbal cues.
- Watch the interactions between work group members.
- Read the emotional states of work group members and observe how they are influenced by situations in the workplace.
- Reflect on your own emotional state and how you are influenced by the emotional states of your work group members.
- Think before you speak.
- Directly respond to the emotional responses of your work group members.

## INSPIRING AND INFLUENCING OTHERS

As a leader, you need to focus on positive emotions that can motivate others. Positive emotions nurture emotional strengths such as enthusiasm, compassion, discretion, broad-mindedness, and optimism.

Negative emotions can lead to emotional weaknesses such as anger, frustration, fear, disillusion, and anxiety. These can have a negative impact on others and your relationship with the team. People are inspired and influenced by leaders who are positive, enthusiastic, and optimistic. Being negative and showing signs of emotional weakness can have the opposite effect.

To eliminate negative behaviors, you need to focus on positive, constructive behaviors.

**Destructive behaviors** trigger negative emotions and provoke defensiveness.

**Constructive behaviors** trigger positive emotions, build upon experience, and provide positive steps for future experiences.

Examples of destructive and constructive behaviors include:

| **Destructive behaviors** | **Constructive behaviors** |
|---|---|
| Judging others | Using active listening |
| Being aggressive | Being honest and open |
| Being sarcastic | Discussing issues and situations |
| Dismissing the opinions of others | Being inclusive |
| Unnecessarily questioning opinions | Being proactive |
| Using personal attacks | Focusing on conversations |

In the workplace, it is essential to lead by example. To achieve this, you should represent the values and standards of your organization, making sure your behaviors and actions are in line with what is expected of you. It is important to show that you can manage your emotions by displaying constructive behaviors and eliminating destructive behaviors. These behaviors and standards should also comply with federal and state or territory legislations and guidelines relating to your organization, regarding issues such as:

- Health and safety
- Sex discrimination
- Racial discrimination
- Age discrimination
- Disability discrimination
- Privacy
- Industrial relations
- Human rights and equal opportunity

Copies of legislation and subsequent updates for each country can be found on the internet. For example, the Australian Federal Register of Legislation is located at **legislation.gov.au**.

# EFFECTIVE COMMUNICATION IN A CULTURALLY DIVERSE WORKPLACE

Achieving effective communication in a culturally diverse workplace requires responding positively to individual workers' differences. This might involve delivering your business messages in several formats to help individual understanding. You must also learn how your work groups perceive the signals you send through your communication and adjust them as necessary. Empathy, or the ability to see things from the perspective of others, is important in order to achieve clear, effective communication.

Some tips for communicating effectively with a diverse workgroup include:

- **Use active listening and focused listening**
  Active listening is a way of encouraging workers to express their thoughts and feelings. It involves paying full attention to the worker as the worker expresses their thoughts, feelings, and emotions. This will lead to a better understanding of their true emotional state. Focused listening involves full concentration on what the person is saying, focusing on their words, body language, and paralanguage, making eye contact, identifying other emotional cues, nodding or

giving verbal cues to show you are listening and understanding, and waiting for the speaker to stop before responding—that is, not interrupting.

- **Build rapport**
  Get to know something that interests each individual and talk to them about it.

- **Use a translator when possible**
  This is especially helpful when working with new immigrants.

- **Ask questions to clarify**
  It is important to ask questions to make sure the person you are communicating with has understood. For confirmation, you could also ask the person to repeat your message back to you in their own words. Avoid closed questions that can be answered with a "yes" or "no" response; use open questions instead. Finally, summarize what you heard.

- **Use appropriate body language**
  Always pay attention to nonverbal cues such as posture, stance, and hand gestures. It is said that about 55 percent of communication is nonverbal. These gestures are often unconscious and so can indicate a deeper emotional state.

- **Choose your words carefully**
  Use culturally appropriate words and terms. Don't use slang or derogatory language, even as a joke. Ask people how they like to be represented, and use language that makes them feel comfortable.

## HARNESSING THE POWER OF THE GROUP

You can help your group have more social cohesion by recognizing the power dynamics that are at play.

Encouraging positive emotions within work groups is a good way to harness the power of your group and help your group to feel comfortable socially. As a member of a work group, you not only need to be emotionally intelligent but you need to be able to encourage emotional intelligence in others, so that the group works well together.

An emotionally intelligent work group is made up of respectful individuals who focus on self-improvement and the improvement of the group as a whole. By doing this, they are better able to manage stress and pressure together and can adapt easily to rapidly changing priorities.

Emotionally intelligent work groups demonstrate empathy and active listening towards individual members, act with loyalty, trust and respect leaders, and solve problems together in fair and equitable ways. These are some ways to help work groups eliminate negative emotions, develop self-management, and achieve emotional intelligence:

- Encourage openness by providing a workplace environment where workers feel comfortable talking about their emotions.
- Act as a role model by demonstrating how negative emotions can be controlled.
- Create online forums where workers are encouraged to share their thoughts, feelings, and emotions free of judgement.
- Give feedback to workers on their self-management skills.
- Set challenging yet realistic goals for workers.
- Be flexible and adaptable at all times, especially in times of change.

## PERSONAL TRIGGERS

It is important to be aware of your own triggers and learn to manage them. Taking the time to develop this self-awareness will give you the confidence to deal with personal emotions and set you on the road to self-management.

Answer the following questions in regard to your personal life:
- What situations trigger negative emotions in me?
- What is it about these situations that triggers an emotional response?
- What types of people trigger negative emotions in me?
- What is it about this type of person that triggers an emotional response?
- Was there a particular action or comment that triggered my emotional response?

- Can I recognize any patterns in the situations that trigger an emotional response?
- How do these emotions present in my body?
- What do I say to myself when negative emotions show up? What is my self-talk?
- How can I respond effectively?

Answering these questions honestly will help you:
- Become aware of your own emotional triggers and how these emotions show up in your body and mind
- Highlight your strengths and weaknesses
- Identify patterns and learn from them
- Gain self-confidence to deal with similar situations in the future

## WORKPLACE TRIGGERS

In the workplace, there are many situations that can trigger emotional responses, including:
- Discrimination
- Perceived favoritism
- Harassment
- Poor leadership
- Poor communication
- Conflict
- Lack of training or coaching
- Lack of support
- Toxic colleagues

It is extremely important that you learn to manage your emotional responses in order to manage these situations effectively and professionally. An important first step is identifying your triggers. To do this, you could ask yourself similar questions to the ones you asked above to identify your personal triggers. Asking these questions will hopefully uncover situations that are common workplace triggers for you.

Developing your awareness in thought exercises like this will help you be better prepared when these situations occur.

Answer the following questions from the previous exercise, this time focusing on the workplace:

- What situations trigger negative emotions in me?
- What is it about these situations that triggers an emotional response?
- What types of people trigger negative emotions in me?
- What is it about this type of person that triggers an emotional response?
- Was there a particular action or comment that triggered my emotional response?
- Can I recognize any patterns in the situations that trigger an emotional response?
- How do these emotions present in my body?
- What do I say to myself when negative emotions show up? What is my self-talk?
- How can I respond effectively?

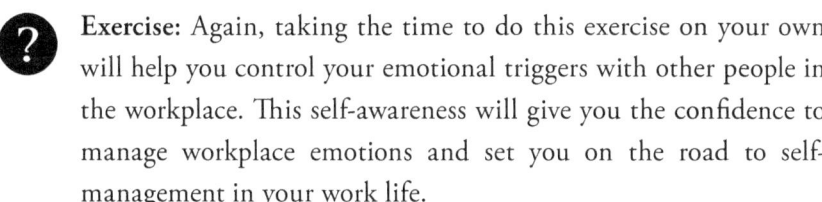

**Exercise:** Again, taking the time to do this exercise on your own will help you control your emotional triggers with other people in the workplace. This self-awareness will give you the confidence to manage workplace emotions and set you on the road to self-management in your work life.

Below are some common workplace situations that can be triggering. Identify any negative responses you may default to in the moment, and then write down the positive responses you could take instead.

Here is one example:

**Trigger:** Feeling that no one is listening to you.
- ✗ **Negative response:** Yell, "You never listen to me!"
- ✓ **Positive response:** Ask for an appropriate time to chat and express your feelings calmly.

**Trigger: Constant criticism**

Negative response: _____

Positive response: _____

**Trigger: An unresolved workplace conflict**

Negative response: _____

Positive response: _____

**Trigger: Feeling unsupported by your boss or manager**

Negative response: _____

Positive response: _____

Analyzing your own emotional triggers and finding positive responses allows you to respond positively when these situations happen. When you have identified your triggers and mastered the emotions they bring up in you, you will find it easier to manage the emotions of others.

## SENSITIVE BUT NECESSARY CONVERSATIONS

*"Kindness is the language which the deaf can hear and the blind can see."*
**Mark Twain**

Conflict in the workplace that is left unresolved—even a simple disagreement between team members—may escalate into avoidance, an inability to work together, verbal assaults, and resentment. In the worst cases, it may also lead to hostility and, eventually, a separation from the organization. Therefore, it is important that the conflict be resolved as soon as possible.

To resolve conflict:
- always be respectful
- be solution oriented
- show willingness to negotiate
- ask a neutral, third party to mediate
- be willing to back down

There are times when sensitive conversations need to be had and kindness is required. Here is a quick quiz to demonstrate how sensitive conversations can be handled proactively and effectively.

1. **Which of the following would you use to start a tough conversation around hygiene?**
   a. "Something stinks."
   b. "What are you doing?"
   c. "Hi, Brad. I've become aware of a sensitive matter relating to your hygiene, and I'd like to seek your help in resolving this."

   *Answer: (C). Be gentle and discreet, but get straight to the point.*

2. **True or False: If an employee doesn't want to address their hygiene habits, they shouldn't have to.**

   *Answer: False. An employer has the right to expect employees to maintain a certain appearance and standard of hygiene.*

3. **Before proceeding with a conversation, be conscious of:**
   a. The prospects of advancement
   b. The consequences of proceeding
   c. Your own agenda

   *Answer: (B). Considering the consequences can help determine whether or not to proceed.*

4. **Difficult conversations can address:**
   a. Policies and procedures
   b. Finance and remuneration
   c. Attitude
   d. All of the above

   *Answer: (D). Many different subjects can be difficult to discuss.*

5. **Active listening requires you to:**
   a. Focus
   b. Use open body language
   c. Be patient
   d. All of the above

   *Answer: (D). All of the above are required.*

6. **True or False: Some people simply do not retain what they are told, no matter what they do.**

   *Answer: False. We can all learn to be better listeners by focusing on the speaker and making a decision to listen.*

7. **True or False: Some people hate to receive feedback, even when it's good.**

   *Answer: True. Some people have had such poor experiences with receiving feedback that they do not want to hear it even when it's positive!*

8. **A performance review or appraisal is an example of:**
   a. Discipline
   b. Interviewing
   c. Formal feedback
   d. None of the above

   *Answer: (C). A performance review is an opportunity to provide formal feedback.*

9. _____ have/has a big impact on what people hear us say.
   a. Negative words
   b. Body language
   c. Volume
   d. None of the above

   *Answer: (B). Your body speaks loudly; make sure it sends the right message!*

10. **Constructive feedback should be delivered:**
    a. In team meetings
    b. In a public place
    c. In private

    *Answer: (C). Feedback should be given in private, with time allocated to address any questions that arise.*

Keep in mind that even if you know the answers to this quiz, you must act on that knowledge to have an effect in your workplace.

# THE IMPORTANCE OF ENGAGEMENT

As I mentioned in Chapter 4, a great leader communicates, energizes, and engages. Although some leaders engage people by projecting certainty, I have always found that the truth is one of the best motivators. When everything is going well, let people know. Tell them why it's going well and what makes it go well, so that they know how to keep making that happen.

We are at work eight or nine hours a day. It would be ideal to feel joyful, inspired, and motivated during this time. Offering opportunities for skill development can improve your team members' work and energy. In my experience, when a team member hasn't completed a certain job or hasn't completed it to the standard that's required, it's not because they don't want to do it, but because they don't really know how. Some people will agree to a task because they want to please you, even if they lack the skill set to do it. As a leader, it is important to recognize when someone needs more training in a particular area. Team members may also want to try out new ideas or progress in their career, and in these cases, it is also helpful to provide training (whether internal or external) to give them the skills they need and keep them actively engaged.

Teams can form temporarily (for example, for one project) or work together on an ongoing basis (e.g., a small firm of solicitors or accountants, administration, sales, etc.); however, all groups need to come to a consensus about what needs to be done and agree on the steps to make it happen. Teams look to leaders to give them that direction, but a good leader will help the team to set their own goals, understand each person's role and needs, and develop a plan for communicating if something is wrong. A Ferrari Grand Prix team is the ultimate example of teamwork—at the Formula 1 Grande Prêmio Do Brasil 2018, Sebastian Vettel had all four tires changed in 1.97 seconds. It was an incredible feat. At any given time, there were eighteen people touching the car, working quickly and efficiently as a cohesive group. A team that works like this needs clear roles and complete trust.

How does a team function with that precision? It starts from the top down. If you are a leader who communicates, energizes, and engages, your team will follow in your footsteps. If you identify any skill gaps, spend time with the team as a whole and complete strength and weakness exercises followed by role play and activities to assist everyone and help them grow as a team. For team cohesion, everyone needs to express the desire to work together and trust in one another. Teams start to fall apart when they don't understand what they're doing, they're not quite sure of the outcome, they don't trust each other, or they second guess without communicating or discussing. Some people find it difficult to trust others. This is where trust exercises help break down barriers and get the team moving forward.

You may have a new team that's discovered a little bit about each other, and you'd like to build trust. The "Blindfold Rope Square" exercise can be a good activity.

**Exercise:** In a furniture-free room, put blindfolds on everyone and ask them to rotate on the spot until they seem disoriented. Quietly place a coiled rope on the floor near one of the participants, and instruct them to talk to each other to find the rope and hold it on the floor in a perfect square. This activity requires a lot of verbal communication and trust. The blindfolds ensure team members can't see each other and must learn to believe and follow what the other person is saying to complete the task.

## WAYS TO ADD ENGAGEMENT TO TEAMS

Using **icebreakers** at team meetings helps workers clear their mind from everything else that has been going on, such as the last phone call with family, something someone said, workload overwhelm, etc. It brings everyone back to the present moment. Icebreakers are a great way to bring fun into the day while making the activity relevant to the meeting so as not to waste time.

You might **start with a great quote** and ask everyone questions like: What does this quote mean? How does this affect our team? How does it help us focus?

Use **trust-building exercises**, such as the "Blindfold Rope Square" exercise I mentioned earlier.

There's a saying, "We employ for will and train for skill." You might have a great team of people who are fully energized and engaged, but if they don't have the skills to do the job, it will lead nowhere. A **training needs analysis** will help each and every person see what they need to progress along their chosen career path. Sometimes we don't know what we need until it's all laid out for us. As a leader, you now have a plan for your team members' professional development. Include yourself in this analysis. Even as the person managing the project, you might need further project management skills to shift your leadership to the next level.

Completing a **SWOT analysis** on the team as well as the project is another great way to come together. This is a great exercise for drilling down and ensuring everyone is in alignment with the project goals and understands where the opportunities and threats lie. Often, one of our biggest threats is our ego, so it is helpful to check in with the group. A SWOT analysis is also a perfect opportunity to reinforce the learning styles of your team members.

The SWOT analysis helps us recognize that every time we identify a weakness, we create an opportunity. For example, if I wasn't great at time management, I could take the opportunity to improve by completing a course in time management (either online or in-person). The next step is to create a planner that I update at the end of every workday, so that at the beginning of the next day I know exactly what to do.

 **Exercise:** Create a SWOT analysis of the team or the project you are working on together. Fill in the table below by listing your strengths, weaknesses, opportunities and threats.

| S<br>STRENGTHS | W<br>WEAKNESSES | O<br>OPPORTUNITIES | T<br>THREATS |
|---|---|---|---|
|  |  |  |  |

This is a continual process because team dynamics and team members' perceptions of the project may change as the project draws out. The moment something does not feel quite right is the moment to take action and address it. Suppose a team member was complaining to a few other project members about a task that the team member had agreed to do at the start of the project. They had thought the task would constitute a small component of their workload, leaving them free to participate in other tasks on the project. However, the task consumed more time than they initially thought, they no longer enjoyed it, and their energy and engagement dropped. The team member may have chosen to complain to their co-workers rather than initiate a conversation with the team leader because they felt it was too late to change. By regularly engaging in activities such as SWOT analysis, team leaders can keep abreast of these types of problems and send the message that changes can be addressed within the project. As can be seen in this example, catching these problems as they arise will greatly improve the quality of the team's work and their enjoyment and engagement in the project.

Conscious leadership means recognizing when a person isn't playing to their strengths or when something is being left unsaid. A quick conversation to ask a team member whether they are enjoying their work or if there is something else they'd prefer, can open the lines of communication and allow the team member to express their feelings. Have these conversations privately, as not everyone is comfortable speaking freely in front of others. If you feel that what they are seeking is outside of the organization, you might say, "Maybe this isn't right for you, and maybe you should look into those areas." This enables them to choose to leave the business and explore a path that makes their heart sing and is better suited to their abilities. If someone does leave, it is important to explain the situation to the team.

I've worked with people who had wanted to be on a certain team, but they didn't fit in and their behavior was destructive. Through having a conversation and being asked, "If you could do anything, what would it be?" they realized that they actually wanted to do something else.

There are times when a team member isn't a good fit for the team; other times they might need further training, or there may be something they need to unlearn. Perhaps someone simply missed a meeting and is not up to speed. But sometimes, the project changed directions, and the team member no longer aligns with it. If you notice a team member is out of alignment, a one-to-one conversation with a simple **values exercise**, such as showing a picture and asking what it means, may help to focus and realign their values.

For example, if one of the values of the organization and the project was "lead by example" (incidentally this is one of Ikea's values), I might choose a picture of a surfer in the middle of a curl. However, if I said, "This picture represents you energizing yourself to be a better leader," the worker may not be able to connect because they can't envisage this. Instead, I would say, "Take your time to look at the picture, and tell me why this picture reminds you of a time when you led well."

The worker can then access their own imagery and meaning. Perhaps to them, the picture represents the perfect balance of getting everything right without the wave crashing and causing chaos, and this reminds them of a time they led well and helps them evaluate their current situation in comparison.

When I was in my twenties, I used to surf every morning. I felt energized and on track. In comparison, in the face of crises like the

GFC and COVID-19, I notice myself feeling a different energy that is based on survival. Looking at the picture, I can easily see that I am out of alignment with my value of leading by example. If I am no longer energized, I cannot be an example to my team. Thus, the values exercise could help me to reinvest in the project and also see what I need to do to get back to my core value—get down to the beach every morning for a walk.

## ENERGIZING YOUR TEAM

Always make time.

Time is one of the hottest commodities today. We can all attest to feeling that there are never enough hours in a day. Yet we've all got the same amount of time as Mother Teresa! It's what we do with that time that makes all the difference. Giving someone your time is valuable not only to them, but to the culture of the team and organization you are building.

## TEAM MEETINGS

Team meetings are a great way to pull everyone together quickly, discuss the project, and fire everyone up! Here are some simple and quick ways to energize your team:

- Hold regular, quick team meetings (fifteen minutes) to let everyone know what is happening across the organization, team, and project, what each team member has on their plate, and whether they need assistance. Ask everyone to identify their three priorities for the day.
- Use a whiteboard and write out quotes to pump the team up.
- Choose a word of the week (or the year). I had big wooden blocks that spelled out CARE hanging on one of our walls to remind us to care for each other, to care for our clients, and to care about everything we did—even washing the dishes to ensure they were clean and dry for the next person to use. Revisiting the word brings it to the forefront of everyone's mind.

There are times we operate on autopilot, which means we are not always leading consciously. What we think we've communicated and what we've actually communicated are different, especially when interpreted through different learning styles. To ensure key information has been delivered, adapt the same message for multiple learning styles:
- Send out the information in a written format such as email.
- Go through the information orally in the team meeting.
- Quiz your team on the information at the end of the meeting (have them repeat it).

The Muse conducted a survey on unproductive meetings and found that an organization spends around 15 percent of their time in meetings, with unproductive meetings accounting for more than $37 billion per year of wasted money![2]

Don't let that happen to you! Harvard studies show that shorter, more regular meetings work best. Keep things relevant and focused on good action and follow-through.

## TEN ACTIONS A TEAM MEETING CAN ACCOMPLISH:
1. Set agendas—establish the tasks, objectives, and time frames for moving forward.
2. Hear feedback—understand what is and isn't working.
3. Build skills—learn from others in the team.
4. Draw on expertise—use the collective mind of the group, as there may be 250 years of experience in the room that can create, discover, or develop something greater.
5. Problem-solve—use the expertise of the team to move around any roadblocks that appear.
6. Pivot—change direction quickly without losing vast quantities of time, energy, or money.
7. Focus—narrow down exactly what needs to be done.
8. Manage—identify the necessary actions to take, who will be responsible, and when they will be completed.

9. Prioritize—set task priorities and assess these priorities as the project changes.
10. Cohere—add in an activity that is fun to relax people and help get everyone on the same page for the shared goal.

## SUPERCHARGE YOUR TEAM MEETINGS

When bringing a new team together, kickstart its cohesion with a specific sequence of meetings:

- **First meeting:** Cover the objective and outcome as well as what's required from each team member and from the group as a whole.
- **Second meeting:** Include a *values exercise* so that team members can align themselves with the project (or choose to step off the team) followed by a *SWOT analysis*.
- **Third meeting:** Start with a trust building exercise.
- **Fourth meeting onwards:** Add a fun activity to the start of each meeting (five minutes), then continue with any organization or team updates followed by project updates.

It's always worth repeating the trust building exercises and SWOT analysis whenever a new team member joins a team to build rapport and cohesiveness.

A lot of people don't spend enough time with this. Imagine you are leading a team of twelve: six have been with the organization and your department for over three years, three have been with the organization for less than eighteen months, two are from another department, and one is new to the company. Every time you bring someone else in, you need to take the time to revisit the foundational exercises so that new team members know the culture, vision, mission, and what's expected of them. And it's a great excuse to have a good laugh during team building activities.

**Exercise:** What three ideas could you implement immediately to energize your team?

.................................................................................................

.................................................................................................

.................................................................................................

.................................................................................................

.................................................................................................

.................................................................................................

## HOW TO PREPARE AN INFLUENTIAL VIRTUAL TEAM MEETING IN TWENTY STEPS

1. Prepare an agenda and ask the team to have their cameras on.
2. Send out the agenda prior to the meeting.
3. Be fully dressed for team meetings as if you were walking into your board room. You never know when you might have to get up and you don't want to get caught with your pants down!
4. Make sure your background is clear or have a flip chart ready for sharing.
5. Open Zoom and check your lighting to make sure your eyes can be seen.
6. Position yourself in the camera so others will see you from just above the waist
7. Check your microphone—can they hear you? Can you hear them? Do a Zoom or webinar test prior to the meeting. The last thing you want to say when opening a meeting is "Can you see me? Can you hear me?"
8. Have a headset handy in case loud noises happen (e.g., thunder or dogs barking).
9. Put a sticker with a smiley face on it beside your camera so you remember to look into the camera and smile when the team comes in.

10. If you are sharing power points, notes, agendas, forms, etc., have them open so that you can choose your item quickly and swap when needed. Have all the materials you want to show ready beside you.
11. Have a printed agenda beside you, and stick to the time frame.
12. Open your room five minutes early, and before you do, jump up and down to get some energy.
13. Preparation is the key, so if you want your team mentally and physically ready, get them to follow the same process. Send them a checklist of these steps!
14. Make anyone who is wanting to share for the meeting a co–host as they come in.
15. Don't touch your face when you are presenting information as it takes your power away (read *The Million Dollar Handshake* to learn more about influence, body language, and business success)
16. When the team comes on, remember to share the agenda and what is required (e.g., how to use the chat and reaction buttons, etc.). Participation is key to any successful meeting, so make sure your team members know why the meeting is important and use a great ice breaker relative to the topic to get their full attention!
17. Remember to look at your camera and smile! Deliver your good points to the camera, and practice delivering bad news just off center (please contact me for stagecraft and presentation advice).
18. A relevant quiz is a fun way to wrap up and make sure everyone is set for what's next.
19. Your tone and pace can inspire and energize people or deflate them—you get to choose. If the meeting is flat, it may be that you did not prepare sufficiently.
20. You have a mute button for a reason—use it!

> *"Always be kind. If you see someone falling behind, walk
> beside them. If someone is being ignored, find a way to
> include them. If someone has been knocked down,
> lift them up. Always remind people of their worth.
> Be who you needed when you were going through hard times.
> Just one small act of kindness could mean the world to someone."*
> **Unknown**

## THE CARE FACTOR

The care factor was a concept I emphasized in our office, and it meant the world to me. If a staff member didn't have the care factor for the team and clients, it was evident in the first few months. Because it is so important to me to create a culture of care—caring for the office, the outcomes, the people, etc.—I knew such people would not fit our values and should move somewhere else.

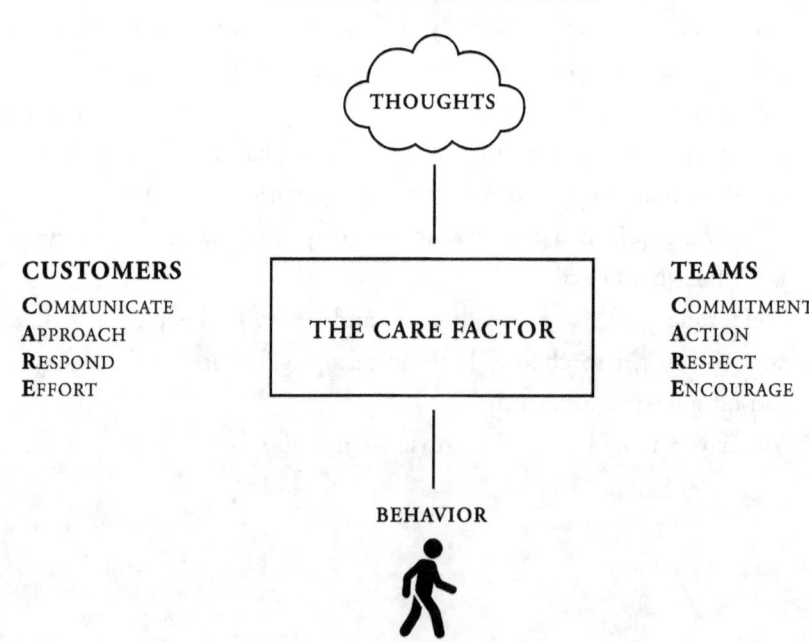

## GREAT LEADERS HAVE A GREAT CARE FACTOR
### PETER BAINES'S STORY

I'd like to introduce you to someone who I believe has a great care factor. He has not only led international teams but has led them through some of the world's biggest crises. His name is Peter Baines. He is the founder of the charity organization Hands Across the Water, but that wasn't what he originally set out to do.

Peter Baines spent two decades as a forensic investigator, unravelling mysteries and uncovering the secrets of criminals. He spent time working with Interpol on counter-terrorism operations in Lyon, France, and advising the United Nations Office of Drug and Crime on counter-terrorism and capacity building. After many years serving at the forefront of international operations, including during the Bali bombings and Saudi Arabia's deadly floods, Peter developed his unique leadership style taking international identification teams into Indonesia and Thailand following the acts of terrorism and the 2004 South East Asian tsunami. It was there, many months after the devastation, that Peter met a small group of orphaned children living in a tent on the grounds of a temple in Bang Muang. Peter believed that if he helped build a home for the children, then some of their problems would be solved. He founded Hands Across the Water and began fundraising.

They built their first home in 2007, and then the real challenges began. They realized that the extent of the problem was greater, and they needed to make a long-term commitment. From its initial thirty-two children, Hands Across the Water expanded across Thailand to help over 350.

In January 2014, Peter Baines was recognized in the Australia Day Honours and awarded the Medal of the Order of Australia for his international humanitarian work. In 2016, he was awarded the Most Admirable Order of Direkgunabhorn by the King of Thailand for his devotion and service to the Kingdom of Thailand.

Peter says, "True leaders are not defined by the position they hold, but by their actions and reactions. In times of crisis or indeed enormous opportunity, it is not the position or title that you possess but what you do which is most critical."

Peter also states that "leaders should not underestimate the value of their presence when it comes to leading." In his travels to communities in crisis, he has seen this kind of presence and the powerful effect it can have.

## PRESENCE MATTERS

*[The following excerpt comes from an interview I conducted with Peter and a portion of his own personal blog.]*

In the aftermath of the earthquake and tsunami to strike the east coast of Japan in 2011, I would spend time with a man by the name of Mr. Sato, who was the community leader of a small seaside village that was destroyed. Lives were lost, homes destroyed, and commerce came to a grinding halt. A number of buildings built high above the water level survived the destruction when those lower did not. Those buildings included a community hall and Mr. Sato's personal home. It was the actions of Mr. Sato each evening that conveyed his understanding and compassion to those in the community he was leading. Rather than partake of his evening meal with his family in his home that survived the tsunami, each night he would make the journey to the community hall to sit and share dinner with those members of his community who had lost their homes.

His presence each evening conveyed to the community that he very much understood their loss and he cared. After the meal, Mr. Sato would move between the group, sitting on the floor next to members of his community to hear of their needs, loss, and generally just demonstrate his commitment to the community.

Mr. Sato did not need to join his neighbors for an evening meal to understand the loss that was inflicted upon his community. He did not provide meaningful solutions during those evening meals as to the reconstruction of their homes or to reduce the burden of the loss of family members. But having the answers is not what was expected of Mr. Sato. His presence conveyed to those he sat next to that he cared and understood—that's all they were expecting of their leaders at that time. There is of course a need for answers to much bigger problems, but the culture of our organizations and communities is often built on much smaller issues.

During crisis and disaster, or with our political leaders, we may not agree with their political persuasions or decisions, and we don't expect them to have the answers and solutions to solve all the problems, but we are looking for presence. For example, during the 2020 Australian bush fires, no one expected the Prime Minister to put the fires out or expected him to have all the answers, but we didn't expect him to be off in Hawaii on a family holiday while the country burned.

Presence is paramount to leadership. Presence shows that you care.

Cath: *Who have you worked with that showed great leadership skills?*
Peter : One person who stands out for me in terms of leadership is a man by the name of Peter Walsh. Peter was an assistant commissioner within my previous workplace in forensics where I spent twenty years, and it wasn't anything about his technical leadership but the way he led that influenced me. I'll just share why by way of example.

When I worked in Tamworth in regional New South Wales as part of the forensic area, I was attached to what was called the Major Crime Squad. My direct boss was located in Parramatta—our team were more like tenants residing in an office whilst our direct boss was in Parramatta. Peter Walsh was also a boss at Port Macquarie, and he looked after Tamworth and some other areas. Whenever he came to the Tamworth Station, he would come into our office to inquire about how we were going. He knew my wife's name, he would ask about the kids, and he had a real concern for our welfare, even though he had absolutely no responsibility for us. Now, the actual boss of the Tamworth Station sat in an office only fifty meters away from my office, but I never saw or heard from him. Because I didn't need to report to him directly, he just didn't enquire or care; he thought, "You don't belong to me. I have no responsibility to you," and therefore, he didn't need to care.

And it's something that's always stuck with me. Peter didn't need to care, but he did. It's about the importance of presence of leaders. Leaders don't have to have all the answers or inspire great change, but when leaders are present, it tells the communities and those that we're working with that they care and understand. And that's what Peter did. He had no responsibility to us, but he would still walk into our office—he would take the extra five minutes and walk up the stairs into our office. He would ask about our life, families, and kids. He asked about work. Now, the conversation would often not be much more than fifteen minutes, but you knew he was genuine. You knew that he cared.

**Leaders are clearly identified by their actions and reactions, not the position they hold.
What we do matters, not where we come from.**

## WORKING WITH OTHERS

Cath: *You have led many teams during crisis. Can you share any insights on working with others?*

Peter: When I held a senior position within New South Wales police and was deployed to handle disaster responses, I often had to pick a team to work with. The process in a disaster response happens really quickly. You have hours to ring people and get things sorted. There's a big processes that happens; the call comes from the Australian Federal Police because it's an international deployment, and then you operate under the auspices of the AFP so they're the lead agency because it's an international event. But a lot of the resourcing gets done through the states. Being part of the leadership team takes a lot of short-term processes and long-term thought processes. For example, it is important to pick the team who not only has the best skills but also could spend months in a tight-knit team living and working under pressure together. Living in tough conditions and working in such a small team, facing significant hardship, requires people who are happy to work long hours and get on well with everyone else. That was one of the most important things for me in building a team—that is, building a smart and harmonious team as opposed to building a team with only the smartest minds.

Team morale and cohesion is important, especially when the stakes are high. It's vital to have clarity of purpose and an understanding of why. It's also important to understand the various stages that people will go through in a crisis and disaster response—it's really just like project management without the warning. There is always excitement at the start and self-motivation. Then frantic natural energy gets you through the beginning stages. After the first or second week, everyone knows what they're doing, and they're feeling a sense of contribution. About three-quarters the way through comes the energy slog. That's when the routine is setting in—you're getting up at the same time to get to the same place to do the same thing. In a disaster situation, you're missing your family, you're sick of work and burnout. The final stage is when you can see the finish line and the morale lifts again because you've nearly made it through and there is light at the end of the tunnel.

Teams need to realize and remember that they will go through these stages and supporting each other will help immensely.

With Hands Across the Water, I didn't see it in stages. In my naivety, I figured that I would provide the children with a home and everything would work out. The kids in Thailand had lost their homes and lost their parents, and giving them a place to stay seemed like the right thing to do. I had a way that I could raise the money to bring about some change, so it wasn't like God said, "Do this," or it was on my vision board as a desire, nor had I ever wanted to start a charity. It was just in response to the needs that were before me. I just figured that I had the opportunity to raise some funds and bring about some change for the kids in need. But later I realized, "Who provides ongoing support for them? Who will feed and educate the kids?" I thought, "Well, this is actually going to take a longer commitment than I first thought." There [were] thirty-two kids within six months; within twelve months the numbers doubled to sixty-four. And what I've seen happen a lot in response to crisis and disaster is lots of people turn up—governments, NGOs, charities, corporates—and say, "We're here to support," but a lot of them leave too quickly. I felt a responsibility to grow our presence and provide the long-term resources. I started to see that providing short-term answers didn't bring about long-term change.

So over time we built more homes in other locations and now support several hundred kids. Each night we have an outreach program to support families so kids can stay within families. We have a university scholarship program and have funded nineteen kids 100 percent of the way through university who are now graduates and working.

But our success at Hands can never be measured in the number of kids that we care for or the homes that we've built. True and ultimate success would be in closing the doors permanently because the need no longer exists, but until that time—until we are not needed—we have a job to do. Our level of success is only possible because of a team, collaborating with great people and businesses and keeping our focus on what matters.

Cath: *You mention great team cohesion. What about those with whom you don't have a great understanding?*
Peter: One of the greatest learnings that I took from working in Bali after the bombings, where the Australian team was charged with the responsibility of identifying and repatriating the 202 souls who had perished, was how to respond with those who had lost their family and friends. The families wanted their loved ones, and we stood between that repatriation process determined to ensure there were no mistakes—but that took time.

The learning I took from spending time with the families was the importance of giving them accurate and timely information. We couldn't remove the pain or provide the answers they were necessarily looking for, and it didn't expedite the identification process, but in communicating in the way that we did—**when you give people information you get their understanding**. To deny them the facts denies them the opportunity to move forward. Dealing with difficult

> conversations in the workplace is benefited by honesty and transparency. It's not always easy, but it pays dividends.
>
> Cath: *What does being a conscious leader mean to you?*
> Peter: Awareness of your environment and the people around you: their needs and their desires. It's about listening and observing and being present.

**Some great take aways from this are:**
1. A conscious leader is present. Your presence matters as a leader.
2. Your actions, reactions, and even lack of action play a big part in whether your people will trust you or not.
3. People can handle the truth. It's not the knowing that causes fear, confusion, and frustration; it's the **not** knowing. Learn to have difficult conversations.

## MANAGING VS LEADING

Managing is ticking all the boxes and ensuring that tasks are completed in the required timeframe. Managers list actions, delegate responsibility, and ensure each step is completed while responding to threats and opportunities as they arise in order to hit the target date.

Leading is how we lead ourselves in any space—walking the talk, and inspiring and motivating our team by allowing them to be confident and certain in what they're doing. As opposed to a manager, a leader develops the vision that propels the project forward. Each and every person on a team has a responsibility to consciously lead themselves.

According to management consultant James Kerr, "There's a difference between leadership and management.[3] Leaders look forward and imagine the possibilities that the future may bring in order to set direction. Managers monitor and adjust today's work, regularly looking backward to ensure that current goals and objectives are being met.

The best leaders lead and let their management teams manage the work at hand."

| Leadership | Management |
|---|---|
| Leadership inspires change | Management guides transformation |
| Leadership requires vision | Management requires tenacity |
| Leadership requires imagination | Management requires specifics |
| Leadership requires abstract thinking | Management requires concrete data |
| Leadership requires the ability to articulate | Management requires the ability to interpret |
| Leadership requires an understanding of the external environment | Management requires an understanding of how work gets done inside the organization |
| Leadership requires risk taking | Management requires self-discipline |
| Leadership requires confidence in the face of uncertainty | Management requires blind commitment to completing the task at hand |

Although it is important to understand this distinction and ensure that your teams are being managed and led, in many cases you may take on both roles. If you are managing, no doubt you will be leading yourself and others too. Remember, the best managers understand how to lead their clients and team members to the results required by the business. Most leaders need to manage, too. In 80 percent of businesses, the leaders of the business are also managing it due to many reasons: cash flow, behavior style, mindset, etc. Applying these two skill sets will not always be easy, but it will definitely bring results. Take the time to understand who is on your team—if you haven't already, go to the Interactive book to find the bonus Behavioral Style Quiz from Chapter 1.

In summary, Chapter 1 described the tool kit you will need to be a situational leader and work in crises and beyond. In Chapter 2, you learned how to manage yourself and others by being a CEIL. Chapter 3 gave you the formula to lead with purpose and set team goals. And Chapter 4 explained how the language you use makes a difference for yourself and your teams. All of these skills are transferrable when leading and managing others.

Be the leader you want to follow. How you behave has a bigger impact than what you say!

**Take the Bonus Behavioral Style Quiz**

On completion, you will be able to download your responses to a PDF. Responses can also be sent directly to Catherine via the interactive book at deanpublishing.com/consciousleader.

**L**    LISTEN

**E**    ENERGIZE

**A**    ACT

**D**    DECIDE

**E**    ENGAGE

**R**    RESPOND

## CHAPTER 6

# THE CONSCIOUS CURRENCY

### THE MICRO AND MACRO OF LEGACY AND LEADING

*"Your legacy is your true currency."*
**Catherine Molloy**

What is it you wish to be known for? What would you like to leave behind for your family or the organization you work for? What impact can you make in the communities around you? These are all considered legacies. We have both micro and macro legacies. Oprah Winfrey famously said, "Your legacy is every life you've touched." Gandhi said, "My life is my message." Business leader Peter Stople said, "Legacy is not leaving something for people. It's leaving something in people."

Aside from "bequeathed gifts of money or personal property," the Merriam-Webster Dictionary defines legacy as "something transmitted by or received from an ancestor or predecessor or from the past." Indigenous people the world over have shared their stories, and passed along knowledge, cultural values, traditions and law to future generations through stories, dance and artwork.

## MICRO LEGACIES

Think of micro legacies as the smaller things that we pass on, generation to generation. It could be as simple as a Sunday family roast. There was a time when our family always came together at Grandma's house for a Sunday roast, and when Grandma died my mum carried on this tradition, and now I love the family coming over for a family roast. Every second Sunday, all the family come together; it's a time for us to sit down and break bread.

My father always said, "Anticipation is better than realization." One of his micro legacies was opening up Christmas presents as a family. There'd be a small stocking at the end of our bed in the morning with something from Santa. Then we would have breakfast with the whole family before passing presents around. Everyone gave a gift to each other; for instance, it would start with the youngest who'd give a gift to everyone, next was my brother, then Grandma, and we'd work our way around the room, and finally we'd open my father's presents last. His saying meant that being excited and waiting could be better than the realization of the present once opened: he liked to create the anticipation of what was possible.

For me, I could never throw rubbish on the ground, and I would be horrified today if my children did this (when they were little, I made them pick it up, quick smart!). These are the micro things we do that can make a huge difference. What do you value? The "Keep Australia Beautiful" and "Clean Up Australia" campaigns started from someone's micro legacy to create a difference at the community level, then they became a National legacy, and now there are clean up campaigns across the globe.

A great legacy can come from small acts of kindness done well. If your family sees you doing things for others (without wanting a reward), then they will want to do things for others also. I do things because I choose to do them and they bring me joy: I never expect anything in return. If you don't expect anything in return, you can't be disappointed. Choose to do things because you want to do them. Create a legacy to pass on to the next generation. If you have nothing nice to say, it is best to say nothing. Create positive and fun micro legacies for the family to carry on.

I came from a family who were conscious of the planet, in what they did and the way they spoke. My father always shut the fridge door once he'd grabbed something out of it. He taught us the importance of conserving energy, thus reducing the carbon footprint on our planet. We had to think about what we wanted before we opened the fridge. (By the way, this is a great way to keep your food at the correct temperature, so its hygienic too.) I've been in other people's houses where the fridge door was left wide open while they poured the drink into a glass, drank it, put it back, and then shut the fridge door. If this is you, just try shutting the fridge door—it takes a millisecond, and most fridges are now self-shutting with just a tiny tap from you. My dad also planted over a million trees in his lifetime and, following the invasive cane toad population in Queensland, he created places for frogs to breed in their natural habitats, making sure the cane toads were kept out. Everyone can make a difference. We are all made differently and have different teachers and experiences in life, so just follow your heart to something you are passionate about and you will make a difference and start a legacy of your own.

In the case of my husband, John's, family, his mother had to feed seven, so there was more scarcity than abundance when it came to food and money. I think it's important that finances are talked about—whether your family had money then lost it, or you're from a family that wasn't wealthy and then made money—there are lessons to be learned. Sometimes we need to unlearn and choose to create new family legacies we want to pass down. Instead of accepting what is, sometimes we have to look at whether the old ways of doing things are serving us. Don't let the HOW in life overshadow the WOW of life. You might want to create a new tradition that your children are involved in that they will want to pass down, or you may want to expand on one that was passed down from your grandparents to you; for example, it could be making photo albums online and sending the printed books to family members. We recorded our grandparents telling stories to remind us of them and for future generations to enjoy. Creating new traditions and making them happen (even if it's a family holiday every five years) are important in order to keep those traditions and legacies alive.

> *"A good man leaveth an inheritance to his children's children…"*
> **Proverbs 13:22, KJV**

When my father passed, I used some inheritance to put aside money for his grandchildren, and each Christmas they all receive money from him to spend. To me, the above bible verse keeps our legacy front and center when we're choosing how to use our money today.

A legacy gives you perspective about what's important to you, which, in turn, leads you to a life worth living.

Being conscious of the little things helps create awareness of the flow-on effects of everything you do and creates a habit of looking at what you're doing; this can also help make you conscious of your actions when in the workplace. Some legacies at work could include random acts of kindness. One of ours was allowing the team to choose which charity we would give 10% of the gross income of the business to each month. We'd also let our clients know which charity we donated to and the amount, so that they knew the effect their funds had on the community (and maybe it even inspired them to start their own giving fund). Another act of kindness could be checking in with your team members regularly, especially in times of uncertainty, and easing the load in times of stress. Another legacy could come from someone admiring the way you lead and the results you get with your team, through seeing your process or maybe even working in your team, and then when they have the opportunity to be a leader, they implement your process with their team. Five of my team members have gone on to make a difference in their communities with their own businesses, and that is just the simple act of paying it forward. Even when you think no one is watching, you are sowing seeds for future leaders.

**Micro Legacy Exercise:**
What are 3 legacies that have been passed down to you?

........................................................................................................

........................................................................................................

........................................................................................................

What 3 legacies would you like to create, improve on and institute personally?

........................................................................................................

........................................................................................................

........................................................................................................

What 3 legacies would you like to create, improve on and institute in your workplace?

........................................................................................................

........................................................................................................

........................................................................................................

> *"What you leave behind is not what is engraved on stone monuments, but what is woven into the lives of others."*
> **Pericles**

## MACRO LEGACIES

To paraphrase a statement attributed to Mother Teresa: "If you can't feed a hundred people, feed one."[1] From her desire to improve the life of just one, she founded the Missionaries of Charity, and at the time of her death it had grown to 600+ missions in over 120 countries, and included hospices and homes for people with HIV/AIDS, leprosy and tuberculosis, soup kitchens, dispensaries, mobile clinics, children and family counseling programs, orphanages and schools.

We've all come across legacies from Nelson Mandela, Martin Luther King Jr., and Albert Einstein, to name a few. It amazes me how they were written many years ago, yet when you read them, they seem as if they were written for today.

There are legacies focused on making the planet sustainable: removing plastic from oceans, saving animals, global warming, climate change, humanitarian work, etc. Anyone can make a difference. It's important to leave the ego behind, be conscious and be of service.

## THE GLOBAL GOALS

In 2015, world leaders agreed to 17 Global Goals (officially known as the Sustainable Development Goals or SDGs)[2], listed below. These goals have the power to create a better world by 2030, by ending poverty, fighting inequality and addressing the urgency of climate change. Guided by the goals, it is now up to all of us—governments, businesses, civil society and the general public—to work together to build a better future for everyone. We have more work than ever to do.

## THE SUSTAINABLE DEVELOPMENT GOALS

| | | | | | |
|---|---|---|---|---|---|
| 1. NO POVERTY | 2. ZERO HUNGER | 3. GOOD HEALTH & WELLBEING | 4. QUALITY EDUCATION | 5. GENDER EQUALITY | 6. CLEAN WATER & SANITATION |
| 7. AFFORDABLE & CLEAN ENERGY | 8. DECENT WORK & ECONOMIC GROWTH | 9. INDUSTRY, INNOVATION & INFRASTRUCTURE | 10. REDUCE INEQUALITIES | 11. SUSTAINABLE CITIES & COMMUNITIES | 12. RESPONSIBLE CONSUMPTION & PRODUCTION |
| 13. CLIMATE ACTION | 14. LIFE BELOW WATER | 15. LIFE ON LAND | 16. PEACE, JUSTICE & STRONG INSTITUTIONS | 17. PARTNERSHIPS FOR THE GOALS | |

## GET INVOLVED

Everyone can contribute to making sure the Global Goals are met. Anyone can change the world for the better.

What's happening around you, and where can you make the most difference?

When we find out where we can make the most difference, it's easy to pass that on to the next person and the next person and the next. Creating a legacy is taking something that's not right, raising awareness and making it so simple that others can help and make a difference as well. When Malala Yousafzai stood up for her right to an education, she wasn't meaning to create waves around the world—she was doing what she felt was right in her heart, and in doing so, she has inspired people all over the world. She is leaving a legacy in the hearts of humanity.

This occurs in business as well. Against all advice from their board of directors, Nike expanded their range to include larger sizes. Nike's purpose is "to unite the world through sport to create a healthy planet, active communities and an equal playing field for all."[3] Two years later, in mid-2019, they introduced plus-sized mannequins into stores with resounding success. It smashed the stereotype that size determined fitness.

A legacy doesn't need to be as big as Nike's or Mother Teresa's. Whether it's a micro or macro legacy, it's what touches our heart that helps us choose what we'd like to contribute to. You may not always be able to contribute financially, but there are other ways to contribute: raising awareness around a cause in your community, volunteering time, giving advice pro bono, etc. Time can be just as valuable as money these days, and often local community charities need extra hands to help out. You could mentor upcoming leaders within and outside of your organization. Being generous with your knowledge is another example of a legacy. You will find that a legacy will fail when people are in it for themselves (ego) or for the money.

When my husband and I went through the GFC and lost nearly all of our personal assets, the driving force for me to build my business was being able to contribute to a cause bigger than myself. Otherwise, I could have been disillusioned with all the hard work and long hours.

I haven't created my own charity because there are so many in the world that resonate with me. For me, it's about giving money and/or time and doing it to the best of my ability. I've always said to my kids, "If you do something, do it to the best of your ability." And know that the best of your ability on one day may be different to your best on another day.

This is where self-reflection is key. With everything you do, ask yourself the following:

*What's working well?*
*What isn't working so well?*
*What needs to change?*
*What changes can I make to create a greater result?*

For me, when you're conscious your domino effect the way you positively lead yourself and others, that's creating a legacy—a currency that we transfer to the next person and so on.

As part of my philanthropy, I was made a global goodwill ambassador in 2017 for supporting causes that are dear to my heart. When I wrote *The Million Dollar Handshake*, I decided to give one third of the proceeds from every book to orphans and mums in Uganda through the charity WATOTO and through S.O.U.P., and with this book, *The*

*Conscious Leader*, a third of the proceeds will be given to The Bombay Mothers and Children Welfare Society.

Another legacy target is to get *The Million Dollar Handshake* into the university curriculum, so that every person can connect and communicate at a higher level of understanding to create win-win results.

> **Macro Legacy Exercise:** What macro legacy would you like to leave or serve? Are there any causes that are of importance to you? (You may choose one from the 17 SDGs above, or just take a moment to think about what concerns you on a global level.) How can you contribute to these? What will you leave for the next generations that will benefit them?

## BUSINESS IS NOT JUST BUSINESS ANYMORE

The United States branch of the business empire PricewaterhouseCoopers interviewed 1344 of the world's top CEOs from over 68 countries about the importance of their legacy. They asked them this question: What is the one thing you want to be remembered for?

Forty-eight percent said they wanted to leave a legacy that grew or transformed their businesses.[4] Many specified things such as pioneering their industry, innovating something new or growing the company in new ways against the odds. Many CEOs also included personal qualities such as honesty, ethical leadership, transparency, and fairness.

To me, this is an indicator that business isn't just business, as some moguls say. Business, and your place within it, is equally personal. Business allows us to create and leave a legacy and simultaneously build our leadership values. For many CEOs and business leaders, this is the playground for building themselves and also for passing on something better for future generations.

One of the longest standing business legacies ever created is Japan's Koshu Nishiyama Hot Spring "Keiunkan."[5] It is the world's most historical inn and appears in the Guinness Book of World Records for this reason: it was founded in 705AD and has 1300 years of history. It has been looked after for generation after generation and stands as a testimony that businesses can endure well beyond your own lifetime.

Business isn't just business anymore; it's about making a difference and leaving a positive dent in the lives of others.

---

*"The legacy of heroes is the memory of a great name and the inheritance of a great example."*
**Benjamin Disraeli**

---

## MOVE UP THE LEGACY LADDER

Just like the ancient pyramids were built from scratch and have lasted thousands of years, so can other legacies—including yours. It doesn't have to be a bricks and mortar legacy…but a legacy that lives in the hearts and souls of others.

When designing your ultimate legacy, you can simply begin at the foundational level with smaller things (the micro legacies), then gradually build to macro legacies…until a greater legacy unveils itself. And if you don't think you have a greater legacy…I can assure you: you do—it's your life.

What we ultimately build is often ourselves, our character, and our leadership skills.

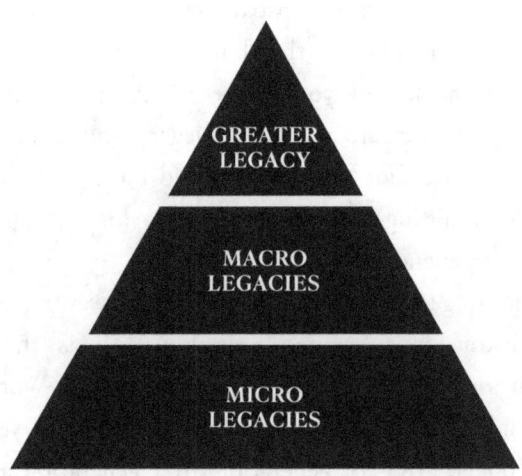

Sometimes you build the legacy ladder by yourself and sometimes you build it with others. My parents built a legacy ladder in the way that they lived. They installed values into us and ensured we knew how to discern right from wrong and to perform charitable deeds. That legacy has been passed onto our children, and thus the ladder keeps going up and up a rung with each passing generation.

Legacies aren't always physical possessions or heirlooms. Many revered teachers left moral and ethical legacies: Buddha, Jesus, Confucius, to name a few. Some writers and ancient scribes left recorded information as a way to inform future generations of healing methods, cultural stories and seasonal cycles.

In fact, every invention you take for granted is a form of someone's legacy. It's something they worked hard on in order to give to future generations. The Romans introduced the world to cement roads, books and newspapers, as well as air conditioning. The ancient Greeks gave us water mills, urban planning, alarm clocks and the Olympics, to name only a few. The Chinese invented soccer, the printing press and the compass. Some awesome Aussie inventors gave us the black box, Google Maps, Wi-Fi and cochlear implants.

As you can clearly see, we all get to enjoy the legacies of generations before us.

## LEGACIES DON'T STOP

The indigenous people of Australia always think generations ahead and learn from the past in order to be conscious in the present. That's why they lived for thousands of years with their families, stories and culture intact before white settlement. They consider the long game. They know that what they do now affects the future generations. Similarly, the Native Iroquois have always been taught to think seven generations ahead (that's about 140 years into the future) and to think of the impact their decisions will have.

Can you imagine the world if we embraced this longevity mindset—if we thought seven generations ahead? The wisdom in this type of thinking is legacy-thinking. It's realizing that what you do now matters tomorrow. That living to consume now does affect the planet and its residents in the future.

The slowest speed is to stop. Just keep taking steps to find out what your conscious currency is; what are you transferring in the world today to impact the future positively? Take the time to find out what's happening, make changes, think generations ahead and speed up. Legacies don't stop…they continue.

Crises don't spoil legacies either. They may delay them momentarily, but they don't stop them. Stay conscious of your long-term vision and legacy through the ride of life, especially during tough or challenging times. Creating a legacy keeps you passionate about life and give you hope for the future.

Even with all of the skills I've learnt and shared over the years, when crises hit, emotions grab the steering wheel out of your hands and sends you into "unconscious-ville." During the COVID-19 crisis, I (momentarily) went through the drama of losing everything I'd worked for (again!). Then I acknowledged it (i.e., it is what it is), looked at how the crisis was affecting others (it wasn't just me; it was happening the world over), how my behavior towards the situation was affecting me (my mindset), and thought about what I could do to change it (mindset, pivot business, etc.).

The key is to keep moving. Every time you hit a crisis, you need to keep going because there will always be an upswing…get ready for it. One of the most beautiful things to remember is disappointment doesn't last, but hope does. The reasons human beings keep surviving are hope and to build a better world for all. During times of crisis, be conscious and ask yourself "What do I want to build, and why?" Do you want your business to remain the same, do you need to diversify your offerings, or is it time to try something new? What is available to you now that you hadn't considered before? What resources do you have, what do you need to learn, and how can your business help others? What's the silver lining, and why?

During the COVID-19 crisis, I found more time for family and for coaching and mentoring groups and one-on-one sessions, which was a great outcome. I've been presented with opportunities to speak with thousands of people online that I would not have had access to previously, and this has opened many doors.

When you believe in yourself, others believe in you too, and this is where the magic happens.

What if every crisis leaves you with more opportunities to be conscious of your impact on the planet, your family and your life? I believe this happens in crises—we assess what's important. After more than 80 flights and 150 stages in 2019, I advised the universe that I wanted more time at home in 2020—and it happened. Big time! Be careful what you wish for…better still always write the goal out!

One of the most beautiful people I've met is Masami Sato. Her heart is massive and her entire business, B1G1.com, is built on businesses leaving legacies whilst simultaneously providing to charities and those in need. This is something very dear to my heart, and it really helps people give what they can and still feel fantastic in making a difference. Many of the B1G1 members wrote a book about leaving legacies, and I was asked to contribute a story to make a difference for our grandchildren. This is part of what I wrote…

# CATHERINE'S ADVICE TO HER GRANDCHILDREN[6]

## BETTER BUSINESS—CREATE CONSCIOUS CONNECTIONS

When you have a purpose, it creates passion; passion attracts attention, attention leads to action and action leads to you growing a prosperous business and life.

When people come together with a purpose, amazing things can happen. When people stop thinking about how they are affected by changes and instead look at the big picture and how they can help others, there's always a positive outcome. Look for solutions and not problems as the business goes through changes.

Positive growth and happiness occur when you are a solution-finder not a problem-finder. Instead of complaining, create win-win situations and a level playing field for all. Everyone is leading themselves to an outcome: consciously make it a good one for yourself and others.

You can create a better business by giving—as you give, so you shall receive. And make sure you laugh and play each day; make your business fun. Train your team in self-leadership.

I definitely recommend that my grandchildren read *The Million Dollar Handshake—How to powerfully connect and communicate in business and life,* by me, which also has online videos and activities attached to each chapter. What I know is that everything will continually change in the world through technology BUT the raw behavior styles of people world-wide are still the same. Learn to consciously communicate—it can save your life and help others.

These simple tools, skills and mindset lead to better business practices and a better and happier life and workplace for all.

## BETTER LIFE—LOVE

I love unconditionally. I look at family as a big tree with long branches, and every now and then you may fall off a branch, but you can climb back up anytime and start again. I was adopted at birth so I was very different to my parents and the family that I grew up in. I was louder, bolder, a risk-taker, but they embraced all I was and I was loved. Being loved unconditionally makes a person feel safe and makes them believe in themselves.

Life is short, and I learnt that lesson at the early age of sixteen when my mother died, and then, before thirty, the mother and father I grew up with were both gone too. They didn't argue or fight, they loved unconditionally and they were always supportive of each other.

I have taken this love with me everywhere I go and so must you. Every person on this planet is unique and cannot be replaced; we need to remember this and treat each other as special.

Some years ago, I took my daughter, Meghan, who was 20 at the time, to visit my birth mother in New Zealand. We met for lunch at a restaurant called 'Soul,' and I asked my birth mother what she would tell her 21-year-old self. She said to take more risks and have more fun. Then she asked me, and I said "Love—love everything—and when you feel really sad, get outside in the fresh air and nature and find something that you love in that moment."

Surprisingly, she then said, "Love is nothing; it's a throwaway word."

I said, "Maybe people throw away what they think they don't love. Maybe they didn't truly love, because love is unconditional—it doesn't judge, expect something in return or create resentment."

We left it at that.

As we packed to leave Auckland and drive to Christchurch, the phone rang. It was my natural mother. She said she had been thinking a lot about what I said, and that I was right…love is all there is! She didn't ever feel loved enough and she didn't love enough—but she still has time.

We all have time to love each other more, to create a better life by loving unconditionally. Every failing you perceive, every goodness that you enjoy, be grateful for each day, because today is the day you get to make a difference. Love someone a little more and have a better life.

## BETTER WORLD
### MAKE A DIFFERENCE AND SHOW THE WORLD YOUR SMILE... BECAUSE WHEN WE SMILE, WE ALL SPEAK THE SAME GLOBAL LANGUAGE

Respect others but stay true to yourself, your purpose, your values and your beliefs; but remain open and listen.

Remember that you are enough. The blessing is in taking every moment you can to make a difference for someone. It may just be as simple as smiling at a stranger. I try to remain truly conscious when meeting people, and aware of my surroundings, understanding how my emotions affect the emotions of others.

Create a better world by being kinder to yourself. Say nice things to yourself and then it is easier to say nice things to others. Surround yourself with people with purpose and passion just like you.

We get one chance at living a better life, at creating a better world. Have fun and just do it.

Love unconditionally.

> *"What you believe doesn't make you a better person the way you behave does."*
> **Catherine Molloy**

Now I'd love you to know more about the founder and inspiration of B1G1, Masami Sato, and what drives her.[7]

## THE CURRENCY OF GIVING
### AN INTERVIEW WITH MASAMI SATO (FOUNDER AND DIRECTOR OF B1G1 GIVING INITIATIVE)

*I was born in Japan. When I was little, I was a very quiet child. Growing up in Japan, being quiet was very convenient. Society and culture expected you to be polite, respectful, humble, and not-so-different from others. If you followed everybody else's way, didn't speak up too much, and stayed respectful, you would be okay. So, I stayed a very quiet child all through my childhood.*

*As I grew up, I wondered why we did all that we did. My parents worked so hard, but when they came home they would often be fighting. I could hear their arguments when I slept and would feel very sad.*

*I wondered why everybody was trying so hard when all we wanted was to feel good, connected and loved.*

*When I finally graduated from college (I studied architecture), I went to Europe just once. I worked really hard and saved up all my money to join this European architecture study tour. To me, the foreign world was something really disconnected from the outside.*

*Without being able to speak any European languages, I experienced moments of amazing kindness. I thought that the outside world was amazing. Maybe I could find a better life and happiness in this outside world because it definitely wasn't here in Japan.*

*My desire to expand my horizons took me on a journey of exploration traveling throughout the world. I traveled to over 25 countries and lived and worked in Canada, New Zealand and Australia before moving to Singapore in 2007.*

*One day, while running a food business, I started to imagine— what if people passionate about education could give back and help educate children around the world. Or the people passionate about the environment could plant more trees as a result of what they were doing. I thought about all my business friends who ran different businesses, they were all passionate about different things.*

*If everybody joined in and gave back through everything we did,* **NOTHING IS IMPOSSIBLE**. *We can solve any problem in the world through our everyday acts because we've got so many people, so many businesses, so many transactions in our world. We just have to be a little more sharing and caring through everything we do. And that's how B1G1 was born.*

\*\*\*

B1G1 is a global business, providing initiatives that makes it easy for business owners to give back and support different great causes from around the world through an online giving platform. Originally founded in Australia in 2007, B1G1 is now headquartered in Singapore, and gives businesses the power to change lives. B1G1 now lists over 500 giving projects from 30+ countries and works with more than 2,500 businesses from around the world. With B1G1, businesses can give back through everything they do in business and create a world full of giving together. Imagine if every time you bought or sold something it made a difference.

While being a mother of two young children, Masami has also been an active entrepreneur. Since 2001, she has founded and led several enterprises and initiatives. I asked her about legacy, and she said she keeps it simple and has discovered that, by nature—if you remove judgment and pre-conceived ideas—humans naturally care and connect.

***

*Growing up I found that I could connect with animals or insects so much better than people. I thought that human beings seemed to often have some kind of disconnect as individual human beings sometimes what we say is not aligned with what we feel. So early on in life, I noticed that people were saying things they didn't really mean.*

*I was quite reserved as a child and didn't talk much because I found it difficult to express myself. The greatest change happened when I started to travel around the world because even though I was still very shy at the same time, I realized that when we let go of needing to say the right thing, or say something in a clever way, we can communicate and interact with people in an easier way—like exchanging smiles or just saying something very simple, like, "Thank you so much for letting me share the food with you."*

*That kind of simple communication really opened me up and I began to realize that we were all more similar than different. For example, everybody that I met cared about their family or cared about the different things that happening around them. So, I noticed a natural and fundamental sense of caring was innate for most people; a desire to extend themselves and connect. When we let go of judgments, pre-conceived ideas etc.... connection happens!*

*Even in business there is often judgement and pre-conceived ideas. Like business owners who are greedy or evil, or the CEOs running these huge corporations that are only interested in making money. But many business owners aren't just in things to line* their own pocket. It's not a swamp of people just wanting to take advantage of others. B1G1 is filled with business owners who want to make a difference not just a living.

What you value is your cornerstone to leaving a legacy and building a business. Our team like to use the DOCARE acronym. D is for Desire to improve, O is for Open-mindedness, C is for Courage. A is for Accountability. R is for Respect. E stands for Enjoyment. These are the qualities we need to for us to be able to do what we do in the best way possible and every team member can continue to improve. For me personally, I like to use three key words: acceptance, trust and love.

Acceptance relates to our past, the conditions we grew up with—so whatever happened in our past, or whatever we see in front of us today, we first must be able to accept it. Because what has already happened cannot be changed, no matter how much how hard we try, we cannot change it. We must accept it.

Trust is more about our future. So, in the future, if we are doubting something bad will happen or you cannot trust this person because he or she may lie or create so much distrust it makes our current experience, less enjoyable. So, it's important that acceptance and trust work together. We must have acceptance of the past and then trust in the future. When we do this…it brings in the emotion of love, which means you will love everything out there.

Now, it's important to note that accepting doesn't mean you don't do anything. Now of course you don't have control about what happened in the past or what another other person thinks or feels—but what you do today is totally under your control. So, by balancing acceptance and trust, allows you to experience joy and love and act in accordance to that sense of love.

Every action we take every day can be more meaningful. If you are coming from a place of love by accepting the past and trusting

> *the future…if something doesn't work out, you can trust that it's the right thing in the long run.*
>
> *If legacies are built on love and you can accept the past and trust the future. Your legacy will sail on the wings of love and live perhaps much longer than you.*

I love the legacy that Masami has created and I love that we have choice. For me, I created a legacy through building a soft-skill training company and have delivered these trainings and systems to some of the richest and poorest people on the planet. Education, to me, is the single most important thing I can do and it is my conscious currency in building a better world and a better life.

## YOUR LEGACY

It's your turn to write your macro legacies and what you'd love to tell your grandchildren about business and life and how to create a better world. Please hand this book chapter on through generations and let them add to it too. To download my free chapter in *Better Business, Better Life, Better World*, go to **deanpublishing.com/consciousleader**.

How I am making a difference in the world?

.................................................................................................................

.................................................................................................................

.................................................................................................................

.................................................................................................................

.................................................................................................................

.................................................................................................................

My conscious currency is...

...................................................................................................................................

...................................................................................................................................

...................................................................................................................................

...................................................................................................................................

...................................................................................................................................

...................................................................................................................................

...................................................................................................................................

...................................................................................................................................

Congratulations—you have acknowledged your legacy. That is the first step to true joy and being conscious of your higher purpose.

When I first wrote this book I was thinking of all the people on this planet that desperately need the wealthier citizens to become more conscious; to recognize how to help and where to spend money in order to clothe, feed and house some of the poorer citizens.

I thought about how the wealthier countries could work with the more disadvantaged countries and consciously come up with worldwide solutions to health, waste and pollution. I imagined all the conscious leaders supporting and nurturing the animals and plants so they do not become extinct. I thought about all the noble efforts that already exist and how incredible and important purposeful people are in sustaining this marvellous planet of ours.

While thinking things through, I realized that it is more important to empower each person on the planet to be that conscious leader, to take up a cause and make a difference in the world. That difference can be as simple as hugging your child. As the quote attributed to Mother Teresa says, "If you want to change the world, go home and love your family."

It is your legacy that you live and breathe no matter your circumstances. You will inevitably make a difference in this world when you are conscious of the purpose you create and lead a life worth living.

---

*"Your conscious currency is your legacy, your legacy is your life, your life is your story, and your story lives on in those that love you...Create a life worth living."*
**Catherine Molloy**

---

# ACKNOWLEDGMENTS

I'd like to thank my husband John, my sons Jackson and Callan and my daughter Meghan who have supported me and my writing journey—another book and four years of book writing, planning and research!

And to my sister Lisa, although we didn't grow up in the same country, we have certainly grown together. I would love to thank you for all the reading, re-reading and for the changes that we made along the way as we edited this book over many coffees, teas and late nights.

A big thank you to all the conscious leaders that have shared their stories within this book—Masami Sato, Peter Baines, Meredith Hellicar, Elaine Jobson, René Deceuninck and Dr. Madhav Sathe. You have all generously shared your stories so that other leaders can learn from your tough lessons and grow through your wisdom. Thank you so much.

To many other leaders that have contributed their stories, content and podcasts to our online learning portal. Thank you for sharing yourself with the world.

To all the positional leaders (political and CEOs) that I have worked with around the globe—thank you for the many insights into traits and behaviors and showing how we can all acquire new skills once we acknowledge the need. Thank you.

To my wonderful friends and colleagues that have been a part of this journey and already booked keynotes and training in Conscious Leadership, I deeply appreciate your feedback and support. Thank you.

A big acknowledgment to Susan Dean and the team at Dean Publishing—you have all encouraged, respected, advised and marketed this book to make a difference in the lives of many people, especially in the way we communicate and help support conscious decisions for the future of the planet. May we make many more CEILs together.

I would like to thank my brother Jason Secto (renowned New Zealand artist and *Lord of the Rings* fame) for the bird drawings and Dean Publishing's illustrator Paul Joy for the Leadership illustrations. You are both incredibly talented and I am super grateful for your contribution.

And a very BIG thank you to you, the reader. Thank you for reading this book, doing the exercises and for seeking to make a difference and become a conscious leader. I love the internal flame that continues to burn from within us all, this drives me to find the simple in the complex. It's the small tweaks in life, when we are conscious of them, that make the greatest difference.

Wishing us all many conscious small tweaks.

# ABOUT THE AUTHOR

Catherine Molloy is an international speaker, Global Goodwill Ambassador and communication expert specializing in leadership, sales and service.

With 27 years of experience in business, training and facilitation Catherine has immersed herself in the fields of communication and body language physiology.

Catherine is the founder and CEO of the award-winning training company Auspac Business Advantage. Catherine has completed her Masters in Leadership and is a Master Practitioner in Neuro Linguistic programming. She is also a qualified DISC facilitator and Is a Gallup-Certified Strengths Coach.

Catherine holds an Excellence Award for 'Regional Business Owner of the Year' from the Australian Institute of Management and was made a Global Goodwill Ambassador in 2017 for humanitarian work in Africa and India.

She is the author of the award-winning book *The Million Dollar Handshake* published by Hachette Australia in 2018 and has been awarded two International Stevie Awards, one for Education and Customer Service and one for Product Innovation.

Catherine is a proud mother of three and lives in Queensland's Sunshine Coast with her husband John and an assortment of animals.

For more information about Catherine and her events and workshops, please visit catherinemolloy.com.au

> One-third of all proceeds from this book goes directly to The Bombay Mothers & Children's Welfare Society's hospital appeal, which helps children survive cancer and provides a living space for their family during treatment.

# ENDNOTES

**Introduction**

1 Molloy Catherine. *The Million Dollar Handshake.* Sydney, Hachette Australia, 2017.

2 The Bombay Mothers and Children Welfare Society, https://www.thebmcws.com

3 Frankl, Viktor E. *Man's Search for Meaning: An Introduction to Logotherapy.* New York: Simon & Schuster, 1905-1997. 1984.

**Chapter 1: Leading Yourself**

1 Microsoft 365. "Introducing Microsoft To-Do, now in Preview." YouTube video, April 19, 2017, https://www.youtube.com/watch?v=6k3_T84z5Ds

2 Wansink, Brian & Sobal, Jeffery. (2007). "Mindless Eating: The 200 Daily Food Decisions We Overlook." *Environment and Behavior* 39. 106-123.

3 Jung, C.G. (1968). "The Philosophical Tree," *Alchemical Studies*, Collected Works of C.G. Jung, Volume 13, Princeton, N.J.: Princeton University Press

4   Dalai Lama (Tenzin Gyatso). *The Path to Enlightenment, translated by Glen H. Mullin*, New York, Snow Lion, 1994

5   Stewart, Greg L., Stephen H. Courtright, and Charles C. Manz. "Self-Leadership: A Multilevel Review." *Journal of Management* 37, no. 1 (January 2011): 185–222. https://doi.org/10.1177/0149206310383911

6   Bryant, Andrew and Kazan, Ana Lucia. *"Self-Leadership: How to Become a More Successful, Efficient, and Effective Leader from the Inside Out"* US: McGraw-Hill, 2012

7   Gallup.com, https://www.gallup.com/cliftonstrengths/en/253958/become-coach.aspx

## Chapter 2: Being Conscious of Emotional Intelligence

1   Davitz, Joel Robert, and Beldoch, Michael. "Sensitivity to expression of emotional meaning in three modes of communication." *The Communication of Emotional Meaning*, McGraw-Hill, pp. 31–42.

Beldoch, M. (1964), Sensitivity to expression of emotional meaning in three modes of communication, in J. R. Davitz et al., The Communication of Emotional Meaning, McGraw-Hill, pp. 31–42.

2   Salovey, Peter, and John D. Mayer. "Emotional Intelligence," *Imagination, Cognition and Personality* 9, no. 3 (March 1990): 185–211. https://doi.org/10.2190/DUGG-P24E-52WK-6CDG

3   ibid.

4   Goleman, D., *Emotional Intelligence: why it can matter more than IQ*, New York, Bantam Books, 1995.

5   Human Performance Technology by DTS, "30 Interesting Statistics on Emotional Intelligence," October 31 2018, https://blog.dtssydney.com/30-interesting-statistics-on-emotional-intelligence

6   Allen, Scott & Shankman, Marcy & Haber-Curran, Paige. (2016). "Developing Emotionally Intelligent Leadership: The Need for Deliberate Practice and Collaboration Across Disciplines:

Developing Emotionally Intelligent Leadership." New Directions for Higher Education. 2016. 79-91. 10.1002/he.20191.

Original source: Source: Emotionally Intelligent Leadership: A Guide for College Students (2nd ed.), by M. L. Shankman, S. J. Allen, and P. Haber-Curran, 2015, San Francisco, CA: Jossey-Bass.

7   Allen, Scott & Shankman, Marcy & Haber-Curran, Paige. (2016). "Developing Emotionally Intelligent Leadership: The Need for Deliberate Practice and Collaboration Across Disciplines: Developing Emotionally Intelligent Leadership." New Directions for Higher Education. 2016. 79-91. 10.1002/he.20191.

8   Goleman, D., *Emotional Intelligence: why it can matter more than IQ*, New York, Bantam Books, 1995.

9   Goleman, Daniel. *Harvard Business Review*. "What Makes a Leader", January 2004. https://hbr.org/2004/01/what-makes-a-leader

10  Rode, Joseph & Arthaud-Day, Marne & Ramaswami, Aarti & Howes, Satoris. (2017). A time-lagged study of emotional intelligence and salary. *Journal of Vocational Behavior*. 101. 10.1016/j.jvb.2017.05.001.

11  Norwich University online, "Emotional Intelligence (EQ) and Leadership." November 3rd, 2020. https://online.norwich.edu/academic-programs/resources/emotional-intelligence-eq-and-leadership

12  Konrath, Sara H., Edward H. O'Brien, and Courtney Hsing. "Changes in Dispositional Empathy in American College Students Over Time: A Meta-Analysis." *Personality and Social Psychology Review* 15, no. 2 (May 2011): 180–98. https://journals.sagepub.com/doi/10.1177/1088868310377395

13  Iniative One™ Leadership Institute, "Emotional Intelligence The New 'Must Have' Skill For Leaders" 30 March 2020. https://www.initiativeone.com/insights/blog/emotional-intelligence-in-leadership

14  Lobbestael, Jill & de Bruin, Anique & Kok, Ellen & Voncken, Marisol "Through rose-coloured glasses: An empirical test

of narcissistic overestimation: Empirical test of narcissistic overestimation." *Personality and Mental Health*. 2016.

**Chapter 3: Lead with Purpose**

1. Sinek, Simon. Via Twitter, June 28, 2013.
2. PwC, "Putting Purpose to Work: A Study of Purpose in the Workplace," 2016 report, accessed February 2021, https://www.pwc.com/us/en/about-us/corporate-responsibility/assets/pwc-puttingpurpose-to-work-purpose-survey-report.pdf
3. ibid.
4. Tony Schwartz and Christine Porath, "Why You Hate Work," New York Times, May 30, 2014, accessed February 2021. https://www.nytimes.com/2014/06/01/opinion/sunday/why-you-hate-work.html.

   Shawn Achor et al., "Developing Employees: 9 Out of 10 People are Willing to Earn Less Money to Do More-Meaningful Work," Harvard Business Review, November 6, 2018, accessed December 2020, https://hbr.org/2018/11/9-out-of-10-people-are-willing-to-earn-less-money-to-do-more-meaningful-work.
5. Edelman. "Executive Summary: Edelman Goodpurpose® Study" accessed December 2020, https://www.edelman.com.
6. CONE: A Porter Novelli company, "2018 CONE/Porter Novelli Report: How to Build Deeper Bonds, Amplify Your Message and Expand the Consumer Base," accessed January 2021, https://www.conecomm.com/research-blog/2018-purpose-study.
7. Patañjali. *The Yoga Sutras of Patanjali : the Book of the Spiritual Man: an Interpretation*. London, Watkins, 1975.
8. Carol S. Dweck and David S. Yeager, "Mindsets: A View from Two Eras," *Perspectives on Psychological Science* 14, no. 3 (May 2019): 481–96, https://doi.org/10.1177/1745691618804166.

   Carol S. Dweck and E. L. Leggett, "A Social-Cognitive Approach to Motivation and Personality," *Psychological Review* 95 (1998) 256–73, doi:10.1037/0033-295X.95.2.256.

9   Agilent Technologies History Center, "1960–Packard Speeches, Box 2, Folder 36–General Speeches," accessed February 2020, https://historycenter.agilent.com/category/packard-speeches.

10  Larry Fink, "Larry Fink's 2018 Letter to CEOs: A Sense of Purpose," 2018, accessed December 2019, https://www.blackrock.com/corporate/investor-relations/2018-larry-fink-ceo-letter.

11  Larry Fink, "Larry Fink's 2019 Letter to CEOs: Purpose and Profit," 2019, accessed December 2019, https://www.blackrock.com/corporate/investor-relations/larry-fink-ceo-letter.

Sara S. Johnson et al., "Editor's Desk: The Potential and Promise of Purpose-Driven Organizations," *American Journal of Health Promotion* 33, no. 6 (July 2019): 958–73, https://doi.org/10.1177/0890117119855446.

12  Domanska, Anna. "What Makes Richard Branson a Great Leader?" Industry Leaders Magazine, 2018, accessed February 2021, https://www.industryleadersmagazine.com/makes-richard-branson-greatleader.

13  Van Gogh Museum of Amsterdam: Vincent van Gogh Letters, Letter number: 274, Letter from: Vincent van Gogh, Location: The Hague, Letter to: Theo van Gogh, Date: October 22, 1882, Website description: Van Gogh Letters Project database of the Van Gogh Museum. (Accessed vangoghletters.org on February, 2020)

14  Statistic Brain Research Institute, "New Years Resolution Statistics," accessed January 2020, https://www.statisticbrain.com/new-yearsresolution-statistics

15  Gardner, Sarah and Albee, Dave, "Study focuses on strategies for achieving goals, resolutions" (2015). *Press Releases* 266. https://scholar.dominican.edu/news-releases/266

16  Vanden, Peter. "How to Set Business Goals," *Inc.com*, https://www.inc.com/guides/2010/06/setting-business-goals.html

## Chapter 4: Language for Leadership

1. Zenger, Jack. Folkman, Joseph. *The Harvard Business Review*. "What Great Listeners Actually Do." Published online July 14, 2016, accessed December 2020. https://hbr.org/2016/07/what-greatlisteners-actually-do

2. ibid.

3. Audio Publisher's Association, Press Release "U.S. PUBLISHERS REPORT NEARLY $1 BILLION IN SALES AS STRONG INDUSTRY GROWTH CONTINUES: Results from the Audio Publishers Association's latest survey shows a 24.5% increase in audiobook revenue in 2018." Published July 17, 2019, accessed December 2020. https://www.audiopub.org/uploads/pdf/APA-Sales-Survey-Press-Release-July-2019-with-2018-Data.pdf

4. Metev, Dennis. Review42. "2020's Voice Search Statistics – Is Voice Search Growing?" Published online November 21, 2020, accessed December 2020. https://review42.com/voice-search-stats

5. Steffens NK, Haslam SA (2013) "Power through 'Us': Leaders' Use of We-Referencing Language Predicts Election Victory." *PLoS ONE* 8(10): e77952. https://doi.org/10.1371/journal.pone.0077952

6. McGinn, Daniel. Harvard Business Review Podcast IdeaCast. "Stopping and Starting With Success." Podcast Episode 560. Jan 19, 2017. https://hbr.org/podcast/2017/01/stopping-and-starting-withsuccess

7. Prnewswire.com. "CEO Reputation Greatly Impacts Consumer Images of Companies, Weber Shandwick Survey Finds." New York, Published online May 2, 2012, accessed December 2020. https://www.prnewswire.com/news-releases/ceo-reputation-greatly-impacts-consumer-images-of-companies-weber-shandwick-survey-finds-149818755.html

8. E. T. Klemmer, F. W. Snyder. "Measurement of Time Spent Communicating," *Journal of Communication*, Volume 22, Issue 2, June 1972, Pages 142–158, https://doi.org/10.1111/j.1460-2466.1972.tb00141.x

9  Chad Murphy, Jonathan R. Clark. "Picture this: How the language of leaders drives performance." *Organizational Dynamics*, 2016; 45 (2): 139 DOI: 10.1016/j.orgdyn.2016.02.008

**Chapter 5: Leading Others**

1  Berg, Paul. "Remember the Needs of Followers During COVID-19", Gallup.com. https://www.gallup.com/workplace/304607/remember-needsfollowers-during-covid.aspx

2  The Muse Editor, "How Much Time Do We Spend in Meetings? (Hint: It's Scary)" The Muse (themuse.com) https://www.themuse.com/advice/how-much-time-do-we-spend-in-meetings-hint-its-scary

3  Kerr, James. "Leader or Manager? These 10 Important Distinctions Can Help You Out." Inc.com, https://www.inc.com/james-kerr/leading-v-managing-ten-important-distinctions-that-can-help-you-to-become-better.html

**Chapter 6: The Conscious Currency**

1  This statement has been used widely and attributed to Mother Teresa, however please note it has possibly been falsely attributed according to her official website courtesy of Mother Teresa Center of the Missionaries of Charity, updated July 19, 2010, https://www.motherteresa.org/missionaries-of-charity.html. I have used it in order to highlight her legacy and demonstrate that small acts can have large impacts.

2  The Sustainable Development Goals. United Nations. Department of Economic and Social Affairs Sustainable Development. "The 17 Goals." Accessed January 26, 2021. https://sdgs.un.org/goals

3  "Purpose," Nike, Inc., accessed 26 January, 2021., https://purpose.nike.com

4  PwC. "Legacy: What CEOs Say They Want to Leave Behind," PwC United States, September 2015, https://www.pwc.com/us/en/services/alliances/ethisphere/ceo-legacy.html

5   https://www.keiunkan.co.jp/en

6   *Better Business, Better Life, Better World: The Movement.* Dean Publishing and B1G1. 23 May 2018.

7   Some of the material used in his interview comes from B1G1 and Masami's personal website. "The Transformation — Masami Sato's Story II." Published online December 15, 2016, accessed December 15, 2020. https://medium.com/@B1G1/the-transformation-masami-satos-story-ii-97ef42530fe

Sato, Masami. https://masamisato.com

www.ingramcontent.com/pod-product-compliance
Lightning Source LLC
Chambersburg PA
CBHW071727080526
44588CB00013B/1929